Call Me Judy

Call Me Judy

JUDY LUCHEY CARTER, ED.D.

PALMETTO
PUBLISHING
Charleston, SC
www.PalmettoPublishing.com

Copyright © 2024 by Judy Carter

All proceeds from the sale of the book will go toward serving the needs of homeless students in the Richmond County School System through the Women In Christ Ministry at Thankful Baptist Church, 302 Walker Street Augusta, Georgia 30901.

Hardcover ISBN: 979-8-8229-4586-9
Paperback ISBN: 979-8-8229-4587-6
eBook ISBN: 979-8-8229-4588-3

TABLE OF CONTENTS

DEDICATION
This book is dedicated to GOD who designed me, ordered my steps, and placed me in my mother's womb. And to my mother who gave birth to me under extremely dangerous circumstances and loved me unconditionally.

FOREWORD

THIS BOOK REVEALS the life from beginning to present of a woman who rose from poverty to achieve recognition from all who knew her well. She is authentic, God filled, and special to many. This book may encourage others who came from similar backgrounds to realize it is not where you come from, but where you are going.

When she walks into a room, time stops, you turn your head and just silently watch. When she walks into a room, she carries a look that is stern, but soft, focused but approachable, business minded, yet reveals the softness of a grandmother and the tenderness of a wife.

Her name had been mentioned in different circles, always with a comment of her dedication to her school and students that she had served. A servant-leader and model of diplomacy, deportment, and discipline. "When she speaks, you had better listen, she does not say much, but that look! She does not play." I feared her, reverenced, and respected her, before even meeting her.

I can recall the first time I spoke with her. I was nervous and scared all in one. I knew she was my sister in Christ, sister in ethnicity, and sorority sister too. However, I was reared to revere wisdom in my elders, and did not want to come across clumsy or foolish. After developing the courage to stop staring at the phone, I finally exhaled and dialed. "Hello, may I speak to Dr. Judy Carter please...."

My world changed in one day, all because of one phone call. Not only did I express my anxiety of wanting to ask her questions about her personal life, but also about myself. Most importantly, she listened, no interruptions, and I am someone who can ramble when nervous or anxious. After I revealed myself to her, she simply stated that she too could empathize with me and my desire to change, be a better person, improve my character development, be more like her. She listened to me first; she focused on my heart not my tone; she shared her testimony, and then allowed me to be her mentee.

She spoke very highly of her mother-in-law Marjorie Butler Carter, and how she listened and encouraged her in so many ways. Soror Marjorie Carter helped her overcome challenges and encouraged her to greater works to begin. I asked her if she would be Marjorie Carter to me, and she said, "Yes" with a smile.

It has been six marvelous years of laughter and sharing, whether it is about oatmeal texture, arranging a dishwasher, or something as simple as using a vacuum cleaner. I am so excited that she finally decided to share her inspiring story with others. She demonstrated to me that it's never too late to change, grow, and be nurtured; a change will come, be patient she said. If she could change me, she can change anyone.

Together, we are still trying to find me a socially acceptable "Laugh." She knows she can call me anytime and I will be there. God works through people, and I am so blessed He chose me to get to know her.

I can call her mother Carter, sister Judy, woman of God, but she just says, "Call Me Judy!"

Marlyn Dobson (2024)

Alpha Kappa Alpha Sorority Sister and Mentee

Chapter One

BACKGROUND
(1942)

"Mother to Son"
By Langston Hughes

Well, son, I'll tell you:
Life for me ain't been no crystal stair.
It's had tacks in it,
And splinters,
And boards torn up,
And places with no carpet on the floor—
Bare.
But all the time
I'se been a-climbin' on,
And reachin' landin's,
And turnin' corners,
And sometimes goin' in the dark
Where there ain't been no light.
So boy, don't you turn back.
Don't you set down on the steps
'Cause you finds it's kinder hard.
Don't you fall now—
For I'se still goin', honey,
I'se still climbin',
And life for me ain't been no crystal stair.

I WAS BORN in McCormick, South Carolina, on June 7, 1942. My name was Judy Carolyn Luchey. According to my mother, I was born breech, at home, feet first. Breech birth occurs when the buttocks or feet appear first during delivery. It is extremely dangerous, as it can cause decreased oxygen and blood flow, and the fetus's head and shoulders may become stuck in the mother's pelvis, potentially leading to suffocation. Most breech babies do not survive. I survived. My mother said that my father and uncle (her brother) were present for my birth. I was delivered by a local doctor and his nurse.

> *"For I know the plans I have for you," declares the Lord,*
> *"plans to prosper you and not to harm you, plans to give*
> *you hope and a future."*
> —Jeremiah 29:11 (New International Version)

McCormick, South Carolina, was a small, rural community, and in my research, I could not find any population statistics for the years 1920–1942. The population is now 2,936. I was told by the records office that the town did not begin keeping records of the population until 2021. I even went to the library in McCormick and found the same problem. Eager to find information about the population, I checked with the capital of South Carolina, Columbia, and was told the same thing. I do not know about now, but McCormick was a corrupt town where all kinds of illicit, immoral, indecent, lewd, and disgraceful activities occurred. I am sorry to say that my siblings and I are the results of that kind of corruption.

In 2003 I needed a copy of my birth certificate to travel out of the country. My husband and I went to the health department in McCormick to get the certificate. I gave the assistant my full name: Judy Carolyn Luchey. She searched for the certificate, came back, and said there was no such person in their files. My husband told her to look under Wideman (my father's last name), and she did. She came back with my birth certificate. I do not understand why my mother gave me her maiden name when my father had signed the birth certificate for me to legally have his name. Because of this mix-up, I was told I had to have my name and date of birth changed on all my legal papers. I was *not born on June 7 but on June 6, 1942.* I changed everything except my last name. I had been a Luchey all my life and did not want my name to be changed to Wideman.

The house in which I was raised was on the property of the white family (the Browns) for whom my mother worked as a maid, cook, house cleaner, and nanny. They owned the house, and my mother did not pay rent. Her salary was $15 a week. She walked to work, as her workplace was close to our house. Our house had a living room with a woodburning stove, two small bedrooms, a dining room with an icebox (not a refrigerator), and a China closet. It also had a kitchen with a woodburning stove for cooking. My mother was a good cook, and we enjoyed delicious meals every day. All the rooms in our house were small. There was electricity but no running water.

We also had an outhouse in the backyard, which served as a toilet. We had chamber pots in our bedrooms at night in case we had to use them. The chamber pots were taken to the outhouse and emptied in the mornings. There was a well in the backyard where we drew water for drinking, cooking, and bathing. We heated the bathing water on the stove in the living room, poured it in a large tin tub, and bathed in front of the stove right there in the living room. We used another tin tub for washing clothes in the backyard and hung them on the clothesline to dry.

The Browns' house looked big to me. It had three large bedrooms, two bathrooms, a large living room, a dining room, a kitchen, and a sunroom. In the backyard there was a hammock where I spent a lot of time in the summer when we were not in school. I went to work with my mother every day during the summer. She let me dust the furniture in all the rooms. My favorite room was the living room. It had a piano, which I pretended to play for hours, even though I did not know a note from a hole in the wall. Someone in the Brown family taught me how to play "Chopsticks," and I played it to death every day. (I am sure this drove my mother crazy.) In my spare time, I would wander in the beautiful bedrooms, imagining one of them was mine. Everything was so pretty. I would think that one day I would have a bedroom like one of those in the Browns' house.

The Brown family was nice to my mother. It was not like the movie *The Help*. We used the bathrooms in their house whenever we needed to, and Mama did not wear a uniform to work. She helped raise all the Browns' children. I played with their grandchildren when they visited in the summer and considered them my friends. One day the senior Browns went to see their son in another South Carolina town and took me with them. I played all day with the children (some of whom were locals). At the end of the day, one child asked if I was an Eskimo, as they had never met a black child before. The Browns clarified that I was not an Eskimo; I was their friend from McCormick, South Carolina.

One of the Browns' sons became a judge, and coincidentally, my nephew, Sonny's son, ended up in his traffic court. When Judge Brown asked his name, he responded, "William Luchey." The judge asked if he had a grandmother and what her name was. My nephew said her name was Willie Luchey. With that said, Judge Brown jumped up from the bench and yelled out that Willie Luchey had raised him. I was told the courtroom was in an uproar. The case was dropped, and Judge Brown told my nephew to never appear in his courtroom again, or he would throw the book at him.

I entered school when I was six years old. At that time there were no preschool or kindergarten programs for black children in McCormick. I was not ready for school. It was a new experience for me. First graders were housed in a little one-room building separate from the main building of the Mims School for Colored Children. We had to walk from our little building up the hill to the main school building for special activities. Looking back, we were lucky and blessed to have such a wonderful teacher named Ms. Johnson. She was so pretty, patient, and kind. We loved her from the first day we saw her. I was excited to start school because I had watched my sister and brother go before me.

On my first day, my mother got up early to make my lunch. She put a sandwich, two homemade fried fruit pies, and an apple in my lunch bag. After two or three hours in class, I felt hungry, went over to the place where our lunch bags were, and retrieved my bag. Ms. Johnson ran over to me and said, "Judy, it is not time to eat now. You have to wait until we all eat together." I quietly put my lunch bag back in place and went back to my seat. I was ready to eat my fried pies, which was all I wanted. I was a picky eater and ate only vegetables, homemade biscuits with molasses, and fried fruit pies. I would give the other things in my bag to my classmates and sometimes the teacher. In those days there were no busses for black children; we had to walk to school. However, in my second year, we were given a broken-down bus that had been used by white children.

I remember learning several things in first grade, such as the alphabet, numbers, spelling and writing my name, how to behave and listen to the teacher, how to follow directions, and how to re-spect both the teacher and other students. I loved Ms. Johnson, my classmates, and the school. Verda Haskell was my best friend from grade one through grade six. (We left McCormick when I finished sixth grade.) Verda was the sister of the Haskell brothers, who were my brother's best friends. I always thought she was smarter than I was, and her penmanship was also better.

Ms. Johnson invited Verda and me to spend the weekend with her at her parents' home in another town in South Carolina, not too far away. I went, but for some reason Verda did not go. Ms. Johnson's parents were so special and nice to me. They let me stay in a pretty bedroom all by myself. Their house was big and pretty. I missed Verda and felt sorry that she did not come on that trip with us. Verda's family was different from mine. She had a mother, a live-in father, and seven siblings. They lived in a big house. I often slept over at her house, and sometimes she slept over at mine. We really loved each other. When I stayed over at her house, I could hardly wait for breakfast. Ms. Haskell would make a big pan of biscuits, a pot of grits, and some kind of meat. She would put a bottle of molasses on the table for those who wanted some. I would always be the first to grab the molasses as I loved biscuits and mo-lasses. I did not care for anything else she made for breakfast.

A special event in first grade was getting ready for picture tak-ing day. My mother took me to her beauty shop to get my hair done. Afterward, she told me how to smile for the picture because I had missing teeth in the front. She told me to smile without opening my mouth wide. I really did not understand how to do that, so we prac-ticed every day until picture taking time. The picture on the cover of this book is my first-grade picture.

In grades two through twelve, all the other students were housed in the main building. Second grade marked my first experience with being picked on (now called bullying). Children called me "cat eyes" because I had hazel eyes. I believe I was the only child in school with hazel eyes. I cried and told my mother about it. She sat me down and told me not to be afraid or ashamed of what the children were saying because my eyes were beautiful. She also told me she loved my eyes and everything else about me. She said never to let other people make me feel bad about myself for any reason. I was told to hold my head up high and know I was as good as anyone else. I will never forget that lesson.

The only other negative experience I remember from elementary school happened in fourth grade. I was not able to recite a poem in class correctly, despite practicing at home with my mother until I got it right. When I recited it in class, I messed up. The teacher kept me after class and had me recite the poem until she was satisfied. By the time I was finished, all the children I went home with had already left on the bus. Therefore, I had to walk home. I lived one and a half miles from the school. As I walked down the road, I saw my mother running toward me. She was crying as she hugged me, asking where I had been. I told her what had happened, and she was mad.

When we got home, she told me she was going to come to school the next day to beat my teacher's butt for keeping me after school. Of course, I was happy to hear that. The next day I told my teacher what my mother had said. Before school was out, my mother walked into the room and told the teacher she wanted to talk to her. I had to wait outside. I tried to hear what they were saying, but they were not talking loud enough. I wanted to hear the beating. When they finished talking, my mother came out and took me by the hand, and we walked home. I asked her about the beating, and she said there was no beating, but she told the teacher if she ever did that again, she would get the beating. I was satisfied. She also told me that I was not supposed to tell the teacher what she said about the beating. I said I was sorry, and from then on, I never had any more problems with that teacher. I continued through grades five and six at that school without any problems, except for the teasing about my eyes.

My mother was a very pretty lady with an imposing figure, shapely legs, beautiful brown skin, and a gorgeous head of hair. She finished high school (eleventh grade) at the Mims School for Colored Children. She made two significant mistakes in her life. However, I want to explain the second mistake first because it involves me: my mother got involved with a married black man in 1941, and I was born in 1942. Even though they were not married to each other, he was present in my life and helped raise me, as complicated as it was. He was always around, except late at night and early mornings, working as a construction worker. When he could not work because of harsh weather or when I was sick, he would sit with me and provide what I needed during the day until my mother returned home from work. He would give me a bell and tell me to ring it when I needed something. He would be in the backyard cutting wood and storing it on the porch or drawing water from the well for us to use for cooking and bathing. I do not think my father finished high school.

When I was four or five years old, he took me to meet his mother, sisters, and brothers. (His father was deceased.) I do not remember seeing any of them again, except for one brother who invited me to spend a week or two with him and his wife when I was in the tenth grade (age 15). They lived in Troy, SC, a small community a few miles from McCormick. That summer, I was raped by a strange man whom I had seen at a place where my new friends and I hung out with other young people. That was the first traumatic experience in my life. My new friends asked my aunt and uncle if I could go out with them, and I was allowed too. They told me we were going to the same dance hall where we had always gone. However, on the way to the dance hall, I noticed that we were going the wrong way. I asked why and they told me that they had a surprise for me. A while later we were in a wooded area, and I began to feel nervous. They stopped the car and that same strange man got in. He told me he wanted to talk to me. I said no. My friends told me to talk to him because he had told them he liked me. They then got out of the car and left me alone with this man. They set this up. This is when I was raped. I tried to fight him off but was unsuccessful. He told me not to tell anyone what happened and if I did, he would deny it and they would not believe me because his family members worked with the police. That night was horrible. My so-called friends took me back home after they stopped at the place where we had been hanging out. I was in pain and did not know what to do. I was also bleeding. The next morning, I told my aunt I was not feeling well, and she gave me something to drink and said it would make me feel better. I did not feel better the next day and told her I wanted to go back home right away. My uncle took me back home in Aiken, South Carolina, where my sister lived. I returned to school when the summer vacation ended and never told anyone what happened in Troy. Several months later, my sister walked into the bathroom as I was getting out of the tub. She told me my stomach looked larger than usual and asked if I was pregnant. I said no. The next day she took me to a doctor who examined me and told my sister I was at least five months pregnant. My sister asked what he could do about it and he said he could not do anything because I was beyond the stage of having a legal abortion. My mother was told, and she immediately said she did not want me to have a baby at such a young age. She asked who did this to me and I said it was a young man at my school with whom I had been out with one time (this was not true). She told my sister and her husband to try and find someone who could perform an abortion on me. They did and took me to this person who they said was well known in the area for performing illegal abortions without any problems. This lady had learned how to do this from her husband who was a doctor (now deceased). I survived this experience, stayed home for two weeks, returned to school and graduated on time. I am asking all young girls who are reading this book to never believe a person who has committed a heinous crime on you. If you are threatened and told all sorts of things are going to happen to you if you tell; tell anyway. Tell your parents, guardians, trusted teacher, principal, or counselor. If I had told someone I could have avoided the trauma and shame of having an abortion. I was blessed to have a mother who never blamed me for the rape. She never said it was my fault. She never made me feel ashamed of myself. She understood. Therefore, I am saying to you; TELL TELL,TELL!!!!

During the time I was absent from school, my friend brought my assignments to me and returned them to my teachers when due. The young man I accused came back to see me when I returned to school and my sister's husband told him to never come back to his house again because of what he had done. I am sure he was confused because he did not know what my brother-in law was talking about.

He never asked me about it, and we never spoke again in school. Of course, he found another girlfriend, and I was hurt.

Growing up, I never knew any grandparents and often wondered what it would have been like to have had them. When I heard friends talk about their experiences with grandparents, I felt sad because I never experienced that kind of love.

My parents were avid fishermen. They went fishing several times a week. I hated fishing but was made to go anyway. The only part I liked about fishing was eating the fish. I still love fried bream and catfish. My father made a fishing pole for me and taught me how to fish. I was not excited about this at all. Sometimes, when we went fishing, I would catch a few fish, and they were excited about it.

When I was about eight or nine years old, I came home from school one day, and my parents told me to take off my school clothes and put on my play clothes because we were going fishing. I was so angry that I slammed the door leading to my bedroom, causing the china closet to fall and break most of my mother's best dishes and stemware. That day I received the only spanking I ever had. (I am sure I should have gotten more, but I did not.) My father went outside, broke a switch from a tree, came back inside, and spanked me. He told me what a terrible thing I had done, and I should be ashamed of myself. After that I still had to go fishing. I pouted the rest of the day and never did anything like that again.

My father was also an avid hunter. He suffered a massive heart attack while on a hunting trip with his best friend in 1954 and passed away at the age of forty-nine. I was eleven years old. It is my understanding that he was never without baking soda, as he thought he had indigestion. He always carried baking soda in his pocket everywhere he went.

Another important aspect of my upbringing was going to church. In the black community, church was held twice a month on Sundays. My mother made sure we were there twice a month, all dressed up in our Sunday best. We learned about Jesus Christ and the things he did for us. Sometimes, I was a little scared that I was not doing everything Jesus wanted me to do and worried about what would happen to me because of it. I loved church and the things we learned about it. I especially liked the Sundays when food was served outside. We could visit all the tables and get what we wanted. My friend Verda and I would have so much fun tasting all the good food. We could not wait until the next time this was going to happen. Verda and I joined the New Hope Baptist Church when we were eight or nine years old. I am not sure we fully understood what we were doing, but our parents let us do it anyway. We were baptized together. Even after my family relocated, Verda and I remained friends.

Verda Haskell, my best friend growing up, as an adult.

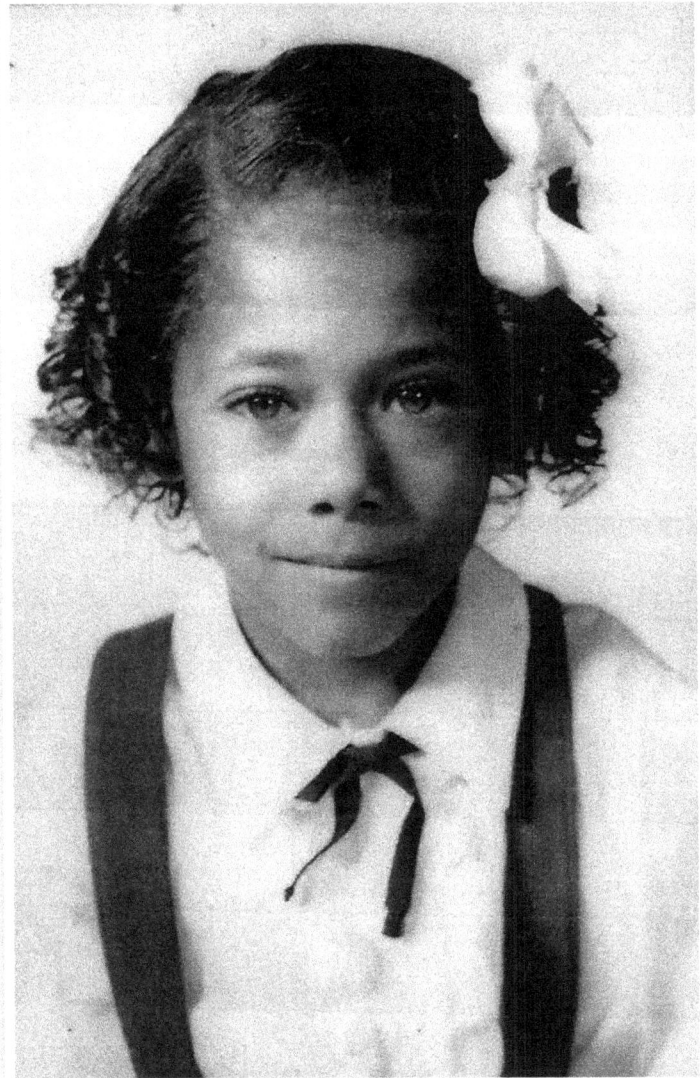

My First Grade Picture

My Fourth Grade Picture

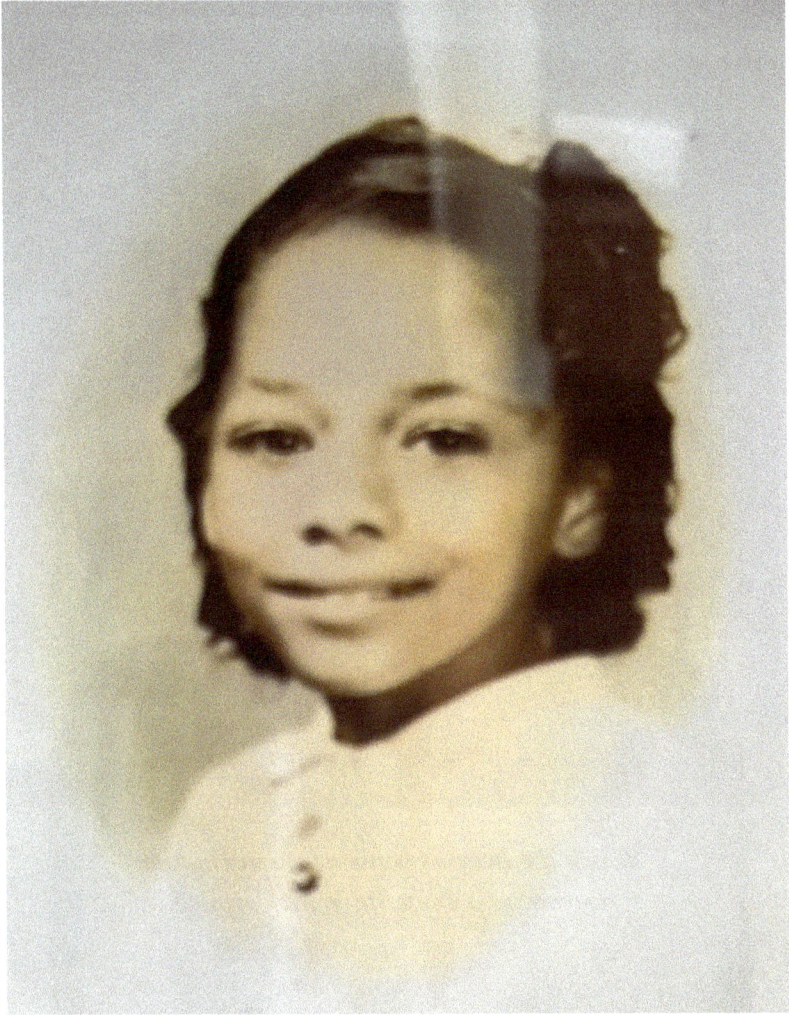

My Seventh Grade Picture

*This is the Brown's house where my mother
worked as a domestic in McCormick.*

This is me revisiting the house I was raised in. It was depressing to see how dilapidated the house had become.

My mother in 1943

Me and my mother in 1942

Chapter Two
MY MOTHER AND MY SIBLINGS—
AN INTERESTING STORY

THE FIRST UNWISE decision or mistake my mother made was getting involved in an illicit relationship with a single white man when she was twenty-one, in 1929. His name was Edward "Ed" McKinney. They had two children, a boy and a girl. This was not a one-night stand but a relationship that lasted eight years. When my siblings were young, their mother was driven out of town by a white mob because of this relationship. She and Ed had broken the law. I do not think anything was done to him. She and her children were slipped out of town and taken to Spartanburg, South Carolina, to stay with relatives until things cooled down.

My sister, Daisy Louise Luchey, was born in 1930, and her brother William "Sonny" Luchey, was born in 1932. Recently, my sister told me she and her brother knew their father and remembered how nice he was to them while they were growing up. She said he visited them often and gave their mother a catalog, telling her to order anything she needed for herself and the two children, and he would pay the bill. She remembered all of them having nice clothes, shoes, food, school supplies, and whatever else they needed.

She and Sonny walked to school every day with other children who lived nearby. On rainy days, she said their father would come to their house, pick them up, and carry them to school. After school, he would pick them up and take them home. I am sure that did not sit well with the white or black community. She said he also took them on casual rides to get ice cream, to the fair, (when it was in town), and to other places. She never said he took them to meet any of his family members. However, some of his family members did know them (a brother, an uncle, and a cousin). My sister said they loved their father and were sad when he passed away. Louise was eight and Sonny was six when their father was killed in a car/train accident.

Both she and her brother were picked on in school (bullied) by other students. They were told to go to the white school because they were not wanted in their school. As my sister explained, most teachers were not nice to them either. Despite the bullying from some students, she had a group of friends who remained close to her even after they graduated high school. She endured discriminatory treatment and graduated from Mims High School in 1948 at the age of eighteen.

As good as my siblings' relationship was with their father (whom they referred to as Ed), his relationship with their mother was another story. My sister told me their mother and father had many quarrels and fights during the eight years before his death. She and Sonny watched in fear, unsure of what would happen to their mother. They did not have grandparents or any other biological relative to take care of them if something happened to their mother. Their father was very jealous and possessive of their mother and did not allow her to go anywhere unless he accompanied her. He watched her like a hawk. He would leave their house, park someplace nearby, and watch their house to see if anyone was going to come there.

One evening one of her uncles stopped by to visit his sister, and Ed thought it was a suitor and shot inside their house with a gun. Her uncle shot back, and both missed. Her uncle was so afraid he left town that night, went to another state (Ashville, North Carolina), and never returned. In those days if a black man shot at a white man, he would be beaten to death or lynched by a mob of white men. That was why her uncle left that night. My sister remembered that night and told me about it recently. Her parents' relationship was so toxic our mother told her when Ed died, it was the happiest day of her life.

That relationship also had a devastating effect on my sister and brother. Because my sister's life with her parents was not exactly normal, she was always nervous, anxious, and scared of everything. She slept in the bedroom with our mother until she got married. I slept on the couch for years, and when Sonny left for the army, I slept in his bedroom. I was never afraid or nervous. The day my sister got married and left home with her husband, our mother waited up all night thinking he was going to bring her back home. She was surprised when he did not bring her home that night. That was the first time she ever slept in a bed without her mother.

My sister, who is now ninety-three years old, married and left McCormick when she was twenty-one years old. She has three lovely children, five grandchildren, and one great-grandchild. She was a homemaker most of her life. When her children married and had children of their own, she took care of her grandchildren while their parents worked, until they finished high school. Her husband of sixty-four years did not want her to work outside the home. He was the kind of husband and father who fulfilled the needs and wants of his wife, children, and later, grandchildren.

After we moved to North Augusta, I lived with them off and on until I was nineteen. I began living with them when I was thirteen because her husband worked at night, and she was nervous and afraid to be home alone. When I was not living with her, I was visiting my mother. My sister hit the jackpot when it came to husbands. He was a good provider who had the old-school philosophy that the man should be the provider, and the woman should not work outside the home. Her husband was a unique person. When he became of age, he worked many different jobs until he landed a job at a South Carolina nuclear plant, known as the Bomb Plant.

While working there, he tried other things on the side. One job was farming. He grew all kinds of vegetables and fruits. When I was thirteen, he taught me how to drive a car so I could help him farm by driving his tractor and combine machine. I would also drive him and the produce to the market when he did not feel well. (Of course, I did not have a license.) He also taught me how to shoot a pistol and rifle. They lived on a large parcel of land with a small forest. This was where we practiced my target shooting. We practiced daily until I got good at it. He wanted me to have this skill because if anyone attempted to enter our house when he was working at night, I would be able to protect us. My sister was satisfied with that arrangement and felt safe. I was driving before my sister learned. She wanted nothing to do with learning how to drive or how to shoot guns. (She was too nervous.)

Another job her husband tried was running a dairy, but that did not last too long. He also tried making moonshine liquor. I helped with that by hauling sugar and ice to the still. Despite being small, he nicknamed me "Splinter", and I was not afraid of anything. The last side job he tried before retiring was making burial vaults. He was highly successful with this venture.

My brother, William Luchey (Sonny), was born in 1932. He lived a troubled life. Recently, his widowed wife told me that he could never accept who he was. He was a very handsome young man who looked white but was treated black. In those days segregation (Jim Crow) was the law of the land, and mixed children were not liked or accepted by white and some black people. People were angry with these children, not the people who made them.

Sonny had two best friends growing up. They were the Haskell brothers (Curtis and Roosevelt). I interviewed them to gather information for this book. They described Sonny as a nice guy with a genuinely nice personality. They said Sonny wanted to be friends with other boys in school, but they rejected his friendship. He was mistreated by students and teachers. It was a teacher who put him out of school when he was in the eighth grade. He played on the baseball team, broke his leg, and was out of class for several weeks, and when he returned to class, the teacher said something insulting to him. When he responded, the teacher told him to get out of her class and school. Of course, our mother intervened, and he was allowed back in school.

His friends and widow told me my brother began drinking when he was thirteen. Alcohol was in our house because our mother sold it to supplement her low salary as a domestic worker. She made the mistake of not keeping the alcohol locked up where he couldn't access it. His friends knew this was how he started because he told them. They told me they tried to get him to stop, but he told them he liked it and was not going to stop. When he was thirteen, he was put in jail for walking home with a staggering gait. A white police officer stopped his car, arrested him, and took him to jail instead of taking him home, even though he lived less than a mile away. My mother's employers bailed him out of jail that time.

He had several other incidents with the law and was arrested. I think if his father had been around when he was growing up, protecting him from mistreatment both in and out of school, his life would have been different. Even though his father was not around, his friends told me that his father's brother and uncle would see Sonny with them, approach them, and ask Sonny if he needed anything. He said when they gave Sonny money, they would give them some also. One of his friends said he had also seen Sonny's father, and he looked a lot like him. It is sad how other family members did not recognize him or his sister. Even today, the younger McKinneys have said they do not know anything about Ed's so-called black children. They do not want to admit they know anything about his black family.

The same teacher who put Sonny out of school when he was in the eighth grade put him out of school once again in his senior year. His friends told me they did not know why, other than the fact that the teacher did not like him. I find it odd that a teacher, instead of the principal, could put a student out of school.

Another problem Sonny had was with white girls. They adored him and wanted to be around him. His friends told me how white girls would go to his house looking for him and how his mother would run them away, telling them not to come back because they would get him in trouble. Our mother was afraid for his life.

The things that happened to Sonny are examples of how difficult it is for a male child to be raised by a single mother. Women and girls need to be more careful about having children with men or boys who are not going to be around to help raise the children when they come along. There are too many males (black and white) in prisons who were raised by single mothers or grandmothers. This is not the way it is supposed to be. Females should think about the outcome of having sex with married men or boys who are just out for a booty call. Females should have better self-esteem and more confidence in themselves and not fall for the lines men have to get them in bed. When you prove your love to them and have a baby, they run on to the next female and pull the same tricks again. Therefore, you are left holding the bag. A single mother raised me, but my father was present in my life, as complicated as it was. That is the reason my life turned out differently.

After the high school incident, Sonny entered the army. My mother had to sign for him because he was only seventeen. She was happy when he left McCormick because she thought that would keep him out of trouble. He served in the army for three years and was discharged for disorderly conduct. The examples I stated above illustrate what can happen to children when they do not live in an established home with both parents present to love, teach, nurture, and protect them. Single mothers face a tough time teaching boys how to become productive men.

When Sonny came home from the army, he dated several girls but married a wonderful young lady in our hometown, Mattie

Harrison. They had a beautiful baby daughter named Turetia (Rita). They lived with us until we all decided to leave McCormick.

———✦———

I would like to make something very clear about our mother. Despite her shortcomings and poor decision-making skills, she was a very good mother to her three children. My sister and I discuss this frequently. She loved us, and we knew it. She made sacrifices so we could have the things we needed. She never abandoned, neglected, or abused us. She never left us hungry, not clothed properly, or with strangers. If she wanted to go someplace, she had a friend stay with us until she returned. She tried to teach us to do the right thing for ourselves and others. She said never to look down on others, no matter the situation. Always try to help when you can. She loved to read and had excellent word attack skills. She served as an usher in church and helped people in the community who were more in need than she was. She visited the elderly, took them food, and often made food for the veteran across the street.

In her meager living conditions and low salary, she always kept an immaculate house and a well-kept yard. She always told us when we were growing up that being poor did not mean you had to wear dirty clothes and live in a dirty house. One could eat off the floor in any house our mother lived in. She cleaned our house so much it smelled of pine and other cleaners. Being clean was so instilled in us that my sister was a perfectionist at keeping a clean house. I tried too but was not as good at it as my sister. Our mother never owned a house, but she took care of the ones she lived in as if she owned them. She took pride in how she dressed and where she lived. I attribute many of my qualities to her.

Our mother continued working as a domestic until her brother was diagnosed with stage four lung cancer in 1973. He lived in another South Carolina town about sixty miles from North Augusta.

He asked her to quit her job and come there to help take care of him. She did and stayed until he passed away in 1974. She returned to North Augusta and lived in the same house until 1976. She then moved into St. John Towers, a senior living apartment building in Augusta, Georgia. She loved this place and was proud to live there.

She was asked to work at the desk, receiving guests, participate in programs, and serve on committees. She was loved by many of the residents and was a confidant to some. In 1989 she developed dementia and could not live alone. My sister and I took her into our homes and took care of her until her dementia turned into full-blown Alzheimer's. Because she refused to eat or drink, and on the recommendation of her doctor, we had to admit her to an extended care facility, where she received great care. Luckily, I was on the board of the hospital that owned the facility.

My sister and I took turns visiting our mother daily while she was in the facility, even though she did not recognize us. She died of complications from Alzheimer's in January 1992. She must have repented and been forgiven for her sins because she was given a few months to live in 1955 but died in 1992. Romans 3:23 (King James Version) states, "For all have sinned, and come short of the glory of God." The Bible also names flawed people whom God chose to do his work. God did not choose people based on their status or wealth. He chose many flawed people who had made mistakes but whom he trusted to do important things for others.

Sonny at 15

Sonny at 17

Louise at 18 – High School Graduation Picture

Louise and Me in 2023

Roosevelt Haskell

Curtis Haskell

Chapter Three

LEAVING MCCORMICK—THE MOVE TO NORTH AUGUSTA, SOUTH CAROLINA
(1955)

WE MOVED TO North Augusta, South Carolina, in the spring of 1955. My mother had been sick for months in McCormick and was advised to move to Augusta, Georgia, to receive better medical care. A relative had confirmed an appointment for her with a well-known OB-GYN, Dr. Agee.

My mother's uncle knew of our desire to move to the Augusta area and informed her of a place she and Sonny should consider. They saw the place and agreed to rent it. Therefore, my mother and I; Sonny and his wife, Mattie; and their firstborn daughter, Rita, moved into the house in North Augusta. The house was so spacious I could not believe we were going to live in it. In my eleven-year-old mind, I thought we had suddenly become rich. The house had too many rooms for us to use, so we decided to use three bedrooms, two bathrooms, the fully equipped kitchen/dining area, and the laundry room. This was the nicest home we ever lived in. There is no picture of this house because the property was sold, and the house was demolished after we moved.

My mother kept her appointment with Dr. Agee, and he ordered surgery right away. The results showed uterine cancer. The doctor told my sister the cancer had spread to other organs, and our mother had approximately six months to live. My sister asked the doctor not to tell our mother because she would not be able to take it. He agreed and said he would continue to see her, follow up on her health, and keep us posted. At that time a minister named Oral Roberts was on the radio, and he said he could heal people through prayer with the help of God. We prayed and sent Oral Roberts a letter, asking him to pray for and heal our mother. My sister received a response from him, which said our mother would be all right. One month after the surgery, my mother returned to the doctor for a review. The doctor told my sister the tests showed no signs of cancer, and he and his colleagues were dumbfounded. He said as far as they were concerned, she did not need any further treatment. She was never told she had terminal cancer.

Mattie's house in North Augusta, SC.

A month later her doctor released her to return to work. She resumed her work as a domestic worker. Her first job in North Augusta was as a live-in nanny for a couple with a baby girl. The couple worked out of town and was only in town a few days a week. During that time they would bring my mother home to spend time with me. She loved that job taking care of the little girl. She did that for at least three years. I do not know why that job ended, but she found another job right away as a maid. She had to work to support herself and me. Her salary was $20 or $25 a week.

Sonny secured a job with the Veterans Administration in Augusta, Georgia. He had received prior training at the VA to prepare for the position of nurse's assistant. He loved that job, but he continued drinking heavily. He never sought professional help for his addiction and later became ill. He was diagnosed with cirrhosis of the liver. His doctors told him he could undergo surgery, which was very risky, or he could stop drinking, get treated, and see how long he would live without the surgery. Sonny chose surgery, had it, lived for two days afterward, and died in the hospital in 1966. He was thirty-two years old. This was a tragic day for his wife and mother. Sonny left his wife with five children, ranging in age from four to twelve. Mattie did an excellent job raising the children. After Sonny's death, Mattie had a very nice house built for her and the children. This was the first home they ever owned. Four of the children went to college, and one joined the air force. After she retired, she sold the house she built and purchased a beautiful home in a lovely neighborhood in North Augusta. Mattie is now living a life of luxury, which she richly deserves.

Also, in 1955, after moving to North Augusta, I enrolled in the seventh grade at Jefferson Elementary School in Bath. The transition from Mims School for Colored Children to Jefferson Elementary was one of the best things that ever happened to me. The school was a beautiful brick building that seemed huge to me. Everyone was nice and friendly. I adjusted right away. I made friends, loved the teachers, and got involved in extracurricular activities such as dance and singing. There was no teasing about my eyes at Jefferson. We had new textbooks, not used ones handed down from white schools, and our buses were not old and broken down. There were so many things to like.

I remember going to the seventh-grade dance with my friend Cecil Stephens. His mother made a corsage for me from flowers in her yard. My brother dropped me off at the school and picked me up afterward. There was a nice cafeteria where we enjoyed tasty food every day, served by friendly staff. Some of the memorable teachers were Mrs. Inez Cook, Mr. Willie Dean, and Mrs. Abelle Nivens. The principal, Mr. A. T. Stephens, was a kind and friendly man who knew our names and made us feel welcome whenever he met us in the hallway or in the cafeteria.

At the end of seventh grade, our house went up for sale. We could not afford to buy it, so we had to move. This was devastating to me. My mother and Sonny found another house that took us back to where we lived in McCormick. This was a double tenement house with three rooms on each side, a living room, a bedroom, and a kitchen. There was no inside toilet. Again, we went back to using the outhouse. A few months after moving in, a toilet and a sink were installed on both sides of the house. We still needed a tub, and later, a tub was installed on both sides. I did not stay in that house too long, as I went to stay with my sister and her family. The school route in both locations was the same, so I could still attend Jefferson.

Mattie, Sonny's Wife

Our second house in North Augusta, SC
(renovated and painted)

Sonny and me dancing 1964.

Chapter Four
MY JOURNEY AT JEFFERSON HIGH SCHOOL
(1957)

I MOVED ON to eighth grade at Jefferson Elementary School, and everything was about the same as in seventh grade. I could not wait to get into high school, where we had watched the older kids in awe. I entered ninth grade in 1957. This was the second transition in my life that proved to be the bedrock for my success. The exposure to learning was phenomenal. The teachers were amazing. We could feel their love for us. They found ways to show us they cared about us and wanted to impart lasting knowledge. They went beyond the call of duty to instill in us the concepts of learning, studying hard, respect for ourselves and others, perseverance, honesty, and commitment.

Some memorable teachers were Mrs. Ruth Ashe, Mrs. Mary Wingfield Bright, Mr. Raymond Dean, Mrs. Eddye P. Fennell, Rev. Nathanial Irvin, Mrs. Fannie Simpkins, Mrs. Thelma Watson, and Mrs. Bertha Williams. Mrs. Ashe taught English to ninth graders and took extra time to teach the girls how to be ladies—how to walk, how to speak, and how to sit. She demonstrated these things to us repeatedly. We all wanted to be like Mrs. Ashe. She was the director of the glee club, and I was in it. She took special interest in me and taught me how to do public speaking. I honed my skills in public speaking by participating in monthly school talent contests, making speeches or reciting poems. I had to practice in front of her before I performed publicly.

Also, during monthly school contests, Annie Willie Bussey, Barbara Samuels, and I formed a group and sang. We thought we could sing like the Supremes. That was a lot of fun. In my senior year, Mrs. Ashe chose me and Sylvester Nabritt to be the mistress and host for the prom. We were so honored to have been chosen to do this.

Rev. Nathanial Irvin taught us history. We never learned history before we learned it from Reverend Irvin. He made it come alive. We learned about the contributions of African Americans to the building of America. We learned about slavery and the inventions of African Americans, the writings, the art, the careers, and other things. His classes were exciting, challenging, and stimulating. We could not wait to get to his class every day.

I enrolled in Mrs. Fennell and Mrs. Watson's Home Economics class where I learned how to bake and sew; sewing was magical to me. Mrs. Fennell took me to sewing competitions in Columbia, South Carolina, where I came close but did not win first place. I loved sewing so much I made some of my own clothes while in high school and after. I ended up baking for all my sister's special family dinners. Mrs. Mary Ann Bright was responsible for my enrolling in college. More about that later in this chapter. Mr. Dean taught psychology, and I loved it. He took the class on a field trip to Columbia, where we visited an institution that housed the mentally ill. He wanted us to see the people we had studied and discussed in class. We saw their living accommodations, spoke with caregivers, and observed clients in different situations. That was my first field experience, and I will never forget it. That field trip sparked my interest in taking my students on field trips during my first year of teaching.

The extracurricular activities available at Jefferson High School were the girls' basketball team, boys' basketball team, Future Teachers of America, library club, New Homemakers of America,

New Farmers of America, student council, patrols, glee club, student bus drivers, annual staff, and cheerleaders. In 1958 the activities added to the curriculum were band, football, commercial education, and industrial arts. I was on the girls' basketball team, but I was not very good, so I only played a little while the skillful players rested. I joined the New Homemakers Club, the glee club, and the cheerleaders. I enjoyed these activities. I was one of the candidates for Homecoming Queen. My mother gave me money to purchase a pattern and material for a suit and hired a seamstress to make it. It was so pretty, and I was proud to wear it. My friend Bea Johnson won. She was a beautiful queen and represented the school well.

Some of my friends were Mary Jones, Maggie Keys, Barbara Samuels, Florence Hatcher, Louise Lamback, Cecil Stephens, Benjamin Prince, Annie Willie Bussey, Elizabeth Mackie, Ernestine Harris, Charles Smith, William Runnels, and Robert Brown. Charles Smith and Ernestine Harris were the smartest students in our class. They loved math and aced every test. I spent a lot of time in the library using the dictionary because I did not have one at home. When I had homework for my English class, I had to drive down the road to Florence Hatcher's house to use her dictionary. I still do not understand why I did not have one in my house. I will never forget Florence for allowing me to come to her house so many times.

While in high school, I wanted to take all business courses but was not allowed to. My teachers told me I had to take precollege courses. I did not want to take those courses because I knew I was not going to college. We were poor, and college had never been an option. We never discussed college in my family. No one in my immediate family had ever gone to college. Some family members suggested I could work in a factory, operate an elevator, or be a cashier in a store. I did not want to do any of those things, and I did not want to be a domestic worker like my mother. So I decided to join the army. My brother found out I was considering the army and told me it was a bad idea for many reasons.

When Mrs. Bright, my homeroom teacher and neighbor, realized I was serious about not going to college, she told me she had attended and graduated from Paine College in Augusta, Georgia, and encouraged me to do the same. She encouraged me daily and talked to me about the importance of a college education. She asked if there was anyone in my family who could loan me the money to attend college. She also said she would get the application for me to fill out. I discussed this with my mother, and she told my uncle Raymond, her brother, about my situation, and he agreed to help. He gave me the tuition, room, and board money to enter college. Mrs. Bright helped me fill out the application, which I submitted and was subsequently accepted. I completed my coursework at Jefferson High School and graduated in May 1960.

A Brief History of Jefferson

Jefferson High School in Bath, South Carolina, was a work in progress. The information compiled thus far enlightens us about the influence of education for African Americans during the nineteenth and twentieth centuries in Aiken County, South Carolina. It is an important history, and we must record our story. It is important for Jeffersonians to fill the gaps of our school's history. Jefferson High School was one of three public high schools in Aiken County, South Carolina, where African American students in grades seven through twelve attended. It operated for fourteen years, from 1956 to 1970. The South Carolina Constitution of 1895, designed to disenfranchise blacks, prescribed a dual system. Black and white students did not attend school together. It was against the law.

The Langley-Bath Colored School was renamed Jefferson Grammar in 1944. The name Jefferson was in honor of Rev. Austin Jefferson Sr., a black minister who was a leader in the community, who advocated for the education of black children. Nine years later, a new school was built up the hill and across the street. It opened in the fall of 1953 as Jefferson Elementary with A. T. Stephens as principal. In 1956 an addition to Jefferson Elementary was built. It opened September 6, 1956, as Jefferson High School. The principal was H. W. Fennell. Jefferson became a school for black and white students in 1970, during the integration of Aiken County Schools. Jefferson High School became Jefferson Junior High School for black and white students. In 1998, this school became Jefferson Elementary School. (compiled by Marsha Fennell Harris, Ed.D., '62).

I am thankful to have attended a school with all black teachers and administrators who cared and were deeply concerned about our overall development. Jefferson is responsible for shaping me into who I am today. The teachers never made me feel inadequate because I was from a low-income family with a mother who was the head of the household. I was encouraged to get involved in extracurricular activities, some of which took me to state-level competitions. The impact the teachers had on my life was phenomenal. I looked up to them and wanted to be like them, and they made me feel as if that was possible. The desegregation of schools was probably necessary, but it ruined education for black children. Black children started going downhill and have never recovered. I am so grateful I never had to attend a desegregated school before attending college. I have heard other black people say the same thing about attending desegregated schools.

Chapter Five

ENTERING PAINE COLLEGE
(1960–1961)

DURING THE SUMMER, before I entered college, something strange happened across the street from my mother's house. Her neighbor, Georgia Bell, an obese, kind, and friendly lady, had a husband, Tom, who was small in stature but physically abusive. He beat Georgia Bell up every weekend. Everyone in the neighborhood heard her yelling and screaming and his cursing and loud slaps and fists hitting her body. One day those sounds started, and after a while, Tom ran out of the house screaming, "I have killed Georgia Bell! I have killed Georgia Bell!" Everyone ran out of their houses and stood around looking.

My mother told me to go inside their house to see if Georgia Bell was dead. She told me that because she thought I was going to be a nurse. I went inside and saw Georgia Bell lying on the floor, eyes closed, and arms stretched out. I felt her wrist and neck for a pulse but did not feel anything. I put my face near her mouth and did not feel any breathing. I went back home and told my mother what I saw. We did not have a telephone, so she ran outside and yelled for someone to call the police. The police and ambulance arrived shortly and took Georgia Bell to the hospital. Someone called later and said she died on the way to the hospital. Her husband was arrested and later served time in prison. We will never forget that day.

Being accepted into college was something I never expected to happen. College was never discussed in my family while I was growing up. This was a miracle happening in my life. I was the first person in my immediate family to attend college. During the summer I continued to prepare for college by purchasing the things I was told to purchase. It was quite an unexpected list. When September arrived, my sister took me to the campus and set me up in the dormitory to which I had been assigned. My room was on the fourth floor, and there were no elevators. I met the three roommates who would share the room with me. The room had two bunkbeds for four people. We got along well.

We got ready for Freshman Orientation Week. What a revelation this was for me. There were so many required rules and regulations. Paine College was a religious school with a strict curriculum, strict professors (of mixed races), required chapel attendance, required vespers attendance, required lyceum attendance, and a strict dress code. Girls could not wear pants on campus and had to dress in church clothes to eat in the cafeteria on Sundays. I could not imagine how I was going to survive in this environment.

As a first-year student, I enrolled in the Lamar School of Nursing Program, which was a four-year program. When I found out I was going to college, my mother wanted me to become a nurse. I had not thought about any career, so I said yes to the one she chose. The black nursing students were housed at Paine College and walked to orientation classes at University Hospital. Our core courses were taken at Paine. Our first experience at University Hospital was discriminatory. The classroom was set up with black students on one side and white students on the other side of the aisle. We did not understand or like that arrangement and let the professors know it. In a few days, the class arrangement was changed, and we all sat together.

The curricular requirements for nursing students at Paine also included courses taught by professors from the nearby Medical

College of Georgia. Most of these professors did not understand how to teach college freshmen and sophomores, and we were not prepared for medical school–level material. Honestly, I did not do well in their classes. They were over my head, as well as some of my peers. I studied hard in groups and alone but did not do well on tests. However, I did okay in regular college courses. I enjoyed the beginning clinical classes very much. I loved interacting with patients, holding their hands, and making them feel comfortable in the hospital. I loved praying with them when they asked. I did not mind helping them in and out of bed, bathing them, and helping them use the bedpan.

What I did not like was having to clean a patient who had defecated in bed and change their linen without moving them. The first time I did this, it made me sick, and I ended up vomiting. I was so ill that I missed class for three days. Every time I tried to eat, I vomited again. The other thing I did not like was learning to administer injections to patients. I could not do it. One day my instructor yelled at me because I closed my eyes while trying to give a patient an injection. That was it for me. I decided nursing was not for me. It was very disappointing, especially since I had made it halfway through, having even participated in a capping ceremony and received our uniforms. My mother was disappointed when I told her I was not going to be a nurse. I am convinced that God's plan was not for me to be a nurse.

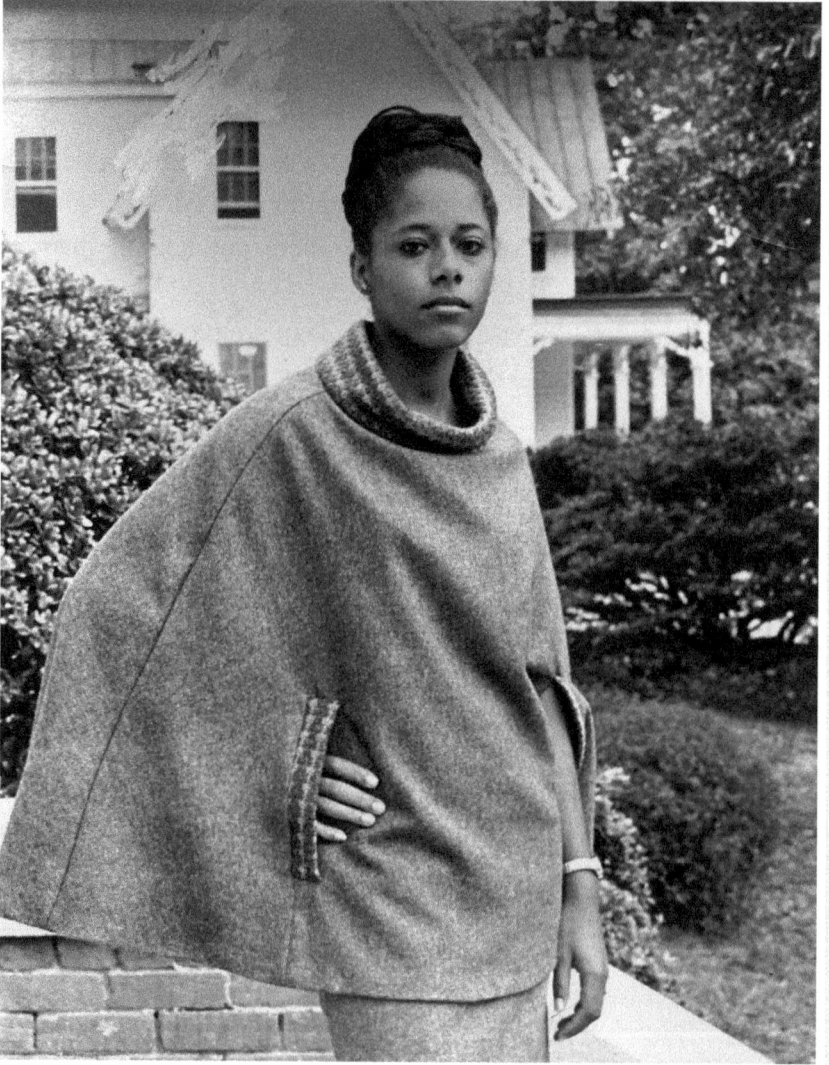

Judy as a Paine College Freshman

Judy in Nursing School uniform, 1961

Chapter Six

MARRYING TOO SOON—A MISTAKE
(1960–1961)

WHILE I WAS a first-year student in college, I met a young man whom I thought was genuinely nice. His name was Mason. He was a sophomore at Morehouse College in Atlanta, Georgia. He wrote letters to me weekly, expressing his love. My friends teased me about the number of letters I received. He came home on weekends and visited me on campus when I did not go home. All my friends adored him, and my family liked him also. He always talked about marriage, but I was not interested in getting married. I liked him, but I did not think we should get married. We dated for a year, and he kept insisting, and I finally acquiesced.

We eloped and married on December 26, 1961. It was supposed to be a secret, and I never told anyone. We continued to live separately with our families until he told some of his friends about it, and eventually, his mother found out. After that happened, I told my family what happened. My mother was extremely disappointed in me, but she accepted it. I was living with my sister most of the time and visiting my mother occasionally to check on her. It was an interesting arrangement after this.

Mason was still in college and came home on weekends. He asked his parents if he could bring me home with him when he came home on weekends. They gave their approval, reluctantly, of

course. When the weekends were over, I went back to my sister's
house, and he went back to college. I was uncomfortable in his parents' house because his mother did not like me. I knew this because
she sent him away one summer to get him away from me to find a
suitable person to date. He told me she said I was from the wrong
side of the tracks and was not an appropriate mate for him. Not
only was I from the wrong side of the tracks, but I was also not
light skinned enough, did not have straight hair, and was raised by
a single mother. Mason's father, a pharmacist and drugstore owner,
and his two sisters, Ethel (fifteen) and Margaret (thirteen), accepted
me right away. We got along from the beginning to the end of our
marriage.

Even though his mother did not accept me, she decided we
should have a reception to celebrate the marriage with family and
friends. It was for her son, not for me. However, she asked my
mother to be responsible for the catering services while she and
her husband took care of everything else. She also made a beautiful
dress for me to wear to the reception. She invited all her friends and
associates. My mother invited her family and a few other people.
The reception was nice, and we received a lot of gifts.

During the first year of marriage, I conceived and gave birth to a
beautiful baby boy, Mason "Skip" III, born on January 25, 1963. He
was so special to me and still is. The first day the nurse brought him
to me, he stared at me with his pretty hazel eyes as if he wanted to
say something. I talked to him, telling him how happy I was to see
him and how I loved him. We were in the hospital for three days and
were allowed to go home. Skip was the first grandchild. When we
got home, Mason's mother surprised me by hiring a lady to come
in and take care of the baby and me for three weeks. Being a new
mother, this was extremely helpful.

Skip was the king of the house. Whenever they heard a sound
from him, his grandmother and two young aunts would race to his
room, almost knocking each other over to be the first to pick him

up. They adored him. Mason transferred to Paine College in 1963 and graduated in 1964 with a major in biology. Skip started walking at eight months, and he started talking in complete sentences at eleven months. In December, when he was eleven months old, he had an accident in the kitchen by pulling a cup of hot water from the table, which landed on the bottom of his face and on his shoulder. We rushed him to the hospital, and he was treated and admitted. Skip was in the hospital for at least a week. I stayed with him day and night. After a couple of days, a nurse came to me and told me to go home and rest, and she would take care of Skip until I returned. When I returned the first day, the nurse had Skip at the nurses' station, talking to the nurses. They were amazed by a child talking at such an early age. Almost every day after that, the nurses wanted to take Skip to meet nurses on other floors. He was released from the hospital before Christmas, and the family had a great Christmas celebrating his being home.

Skip at 11 months when he was released from the hospital

Skips Paternal Grandparents

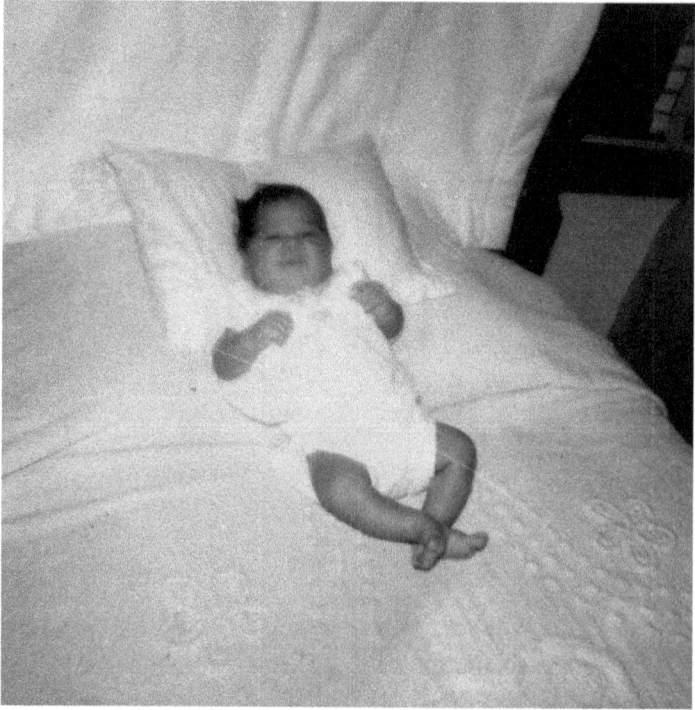

Skip as a baby

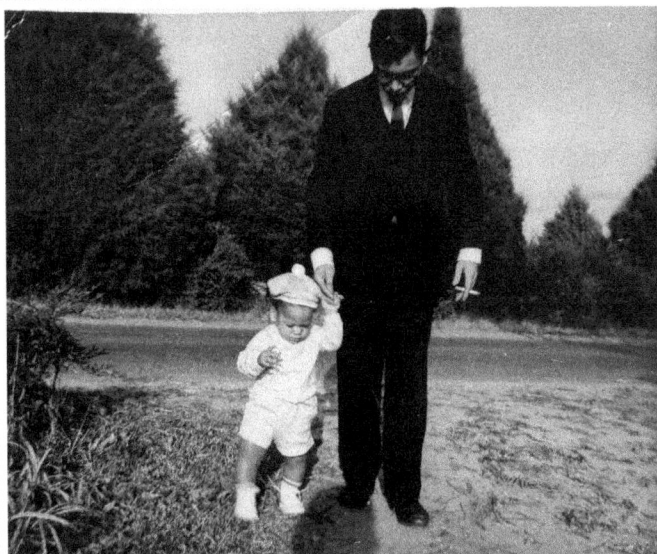

Skip and Father, Mason

Chapter Seven
DESTROYING A MARRIAGE

AFTER A YEAR of living with his parents, we moved into an apartment. Things were okay the first year when we were living with Mason's parents, but problems began when we moved. I did not know Mason was more than a social drinker before we were married. I was told after we married that he had started drinking in high school. Being on our own gave him the opportunity to drink more. However, he got a job teaching biology in a local elementary school.

I stayed home with Skip and waited until he was two years old before he could enter day care. Mason provided for us financially but not emotionally. We had food, clothing, comfortable housing, and all other necessities of life, except his attention. Skip and I spent our days learning colors, naming the parts of the body, and other baby things. We went for walks and talked about what we saw. We spent a lot of time together those two years.

Mason began drinking from morning to night. He did not spend any time with the baby and me. He left his job, went drinking, and would come home at two or three in the morning. We would fuss and yell at each other until we were exhausted. He lost his first job because he was caught drinking on the job. He got another job and lost it for the same reason. Early one morning he came home while I was finishing a paper for an art class. We argued about something, and he got mad and set my paper on fire. My art professor was nice enough to let me turn the paper in a day late. However, my grade was changed from an A to a B.

At this time his father hired him to work in his pharmacy. Our marital problems got worse. He added infidelity and physical abuse to his problems. He began hitting me and pulling his pistol on me. I admit I fought back but never called the police because I did not want him to have a criminal record. Through all our fighting, Skip never woke up from sleeping. That was a blessing.

When Skip entered day care, I returned to Paine College in 1964 (spring semester) to complete my education. Mason's mother paid for my tuition because she had encouraged me to return to college. The marital problems did not get any better, so I left one night after an abusive fight. I did not want to let my mother or sister know what I had done because I knew my mother would make me come home with her. She was very serious about any abuse toward her daughters. My baby and I stayed in my car the night I left. The next day I went to the Dean of Women, Ms. Blount, at Paine and informed her of my situation. She told me that my baby and I could stay in the girls' dormitory for as long as needed.

Mrs. Freddie P. Jackson, the lady who ran the cafeteria, allowed Skip and me to eat there for free. My friends took turns taking care of Skip while I attended my classes. It was fortunate to have a place to stay, but it was difficult to manage classes, study, and take care of my baby in a dormitory. It was such a blessing to have friends come to my aid. Eventually, I told Mason where we were, and he came over begging me to return, promising he would change. I refused for a month then went back. I went back because I did not want our son to be raised without his biological father or by a single mother.

Things were better for a while, then the same problems began again, only escalating. This time I stayed until April 17, 1967. That night Mason came home around 2:30 a.m., drunk and angry with me because I questioned his behavior. He attacked me, and we fought.

I told him I was going to leave again and never come back. (Never tell a man you are going to leave; just do it.) He went to another room, retrieved his pistol, came back, and put the loaded pistol to my head and said I was not going to leave him because he was going to blow my brains out right then. I was so scared; I did not know what to do. Something told me to take the pistol from him. We struggled with the loaded pistol, and I finally gained control of it. I then started beating him over his head with the handle of the pistol.

When I saw blood running down his face, I panicked, threw the pistol down, and ran out of the house barefoot in my nightgown. I thought he was behind me. I ran through neighbors' yards, getting all cut and scratched up by shrubbery and bushes. I ran for almost a block until I arrived at his uncle and aunt's house. I banged on the door, and they let me in, asking what was wrong. I explained what had happened, and they said, "We will take you back to the house to get the baby." I said I was afraid to go back, and I was not going until my mother came to get me.

I called my sister-in-law, and she brought my mother to get me in less than an hour. We went back to our house, and Mason was sitting in a chair with a bloody towel wrapped around his head. My mother asked him why he was abusing me and what was wrong with him. His response was, "She is my wife, and I can do whatever I want to her."

My mother pulled a pistol out of her purse, pointed it at his head, and said, "If you ever touch my baby again, I will blow your brains out." He did not say another word to her. She told me to gather a few things for the baby and myself and come back later for the rest. We were going home with her in North Augusta.

The next day my sister took me back to Aiken, South Carolina, to meet an attorney. He listened to my problem, asked a lot of questions, and took pictures of my body. After our discussion, he told me he had enough evidence for me to file for divorce and be eligible for alimony, child support, and his fees to be paid by my husband.

I told him I did not want alimony, only child support and his fees. He tried to convince me otherwise, but I refused. The divorce was finalized on July 25, 1967. Before the divorce was finalized, Mason came begging back again. I refused to give in. One day he even came to the house with a new car, saying it was for me. I replied that if it was truly for me, he should give me the keys. He said he would give me the keys when I came back. That day I made it clear to him that nothing could convince me to return to the trauma I had experienced for almost six years. He finally believed me and remarried shortly afterward.

He joined the navy, served several years, and retired in California. He did not have contact with our son during those years. The only time he saw Skip was when he visited his parents and Skip was there. When our son graduated college (as an honor graduate), he wrote him a letter apologizing for not being a good father and admitted that alcohol was the problem. He left California a few years ago and moved back to his birthplace. He had lung cancer and was dying. At the request of his father, Skip went to see him a couple of times but told me the meetings were awkward because they really did not know each other. Mason passed away in 2020.

Before he passed away, I forgave him for the way he mistreated me and his son because I realized it was because of his addiction, something he could not control. He was offered help by his parents, but he refused. He had become a person who was different from the man I married. I was sorry that he missed witnessing his son grow from a smart child into a handsome, brilliant, confident, God-blessed, and successful young man. My son is an amazing person, and I am super proud of him. After graduating from college as a Presidential Scholar (full scholarship), he was accepted into medical school. He decided the first year he did not like it and wanted to leave. I did not try to change his mind. He left and resigned his seat.

During the summer the dean called and asked why he resigned. My husband told him it was because he was not happy there and thought he might have made a mistake. The dean said Skip was doing well and suggested he give it another try. Skip decided to return for his sophomore year. He did not like it any better and resigned at the end of the year. He underwent testing and was hired at the Savannah River Site, a nuclear plant in South Carolina, where he has remained for thirty-five years. During those years he was promoted to upper-level positions and settled in the training (teaching/instructor) area. He has the reputation of being one of the best instructors on-site.

Back to separating from Mason for the last time. I had just begun my last semester of college in the student teaching experience before I left that relationship for good. After leaving, I did not have transportation to go to work. I had left abruptly without my car, which had been given to me by Mason, and he was not going to give it back to me unless I returned. I called a former high school teacher, Mrs. Fannie S. Johnson, who lived near my mother, asking if she could pick me up and drop me off on her way to work. She kindly agreed, but I still had to find a way back home as our school closing times were different. I really needed a car, so I asked my uncle Raymond to loan me $250 to purchase a used Volkswagen, and once again he came to my rescue.

My mother paid a neighbor to take care of Skip while I was student teaching and she was working. This living situation was not easy on any of us. My mother had only one bedroom in her house. Skip slept with my mother, and I slept on the couch in the living room. It was hard for her to feed us on her tiny salary of $25 a week. However, she never complained. She managed to pay her rent, buy food, and put money in the basket at church.

Skip Receiving the President's Award from the Savannah River Site (SR5) for his contributions to the facility.

Skip in his Easter suite, Age 5

*Skip after his induction into the Omega Psi Phi
Fraternity at South Carolina State University*

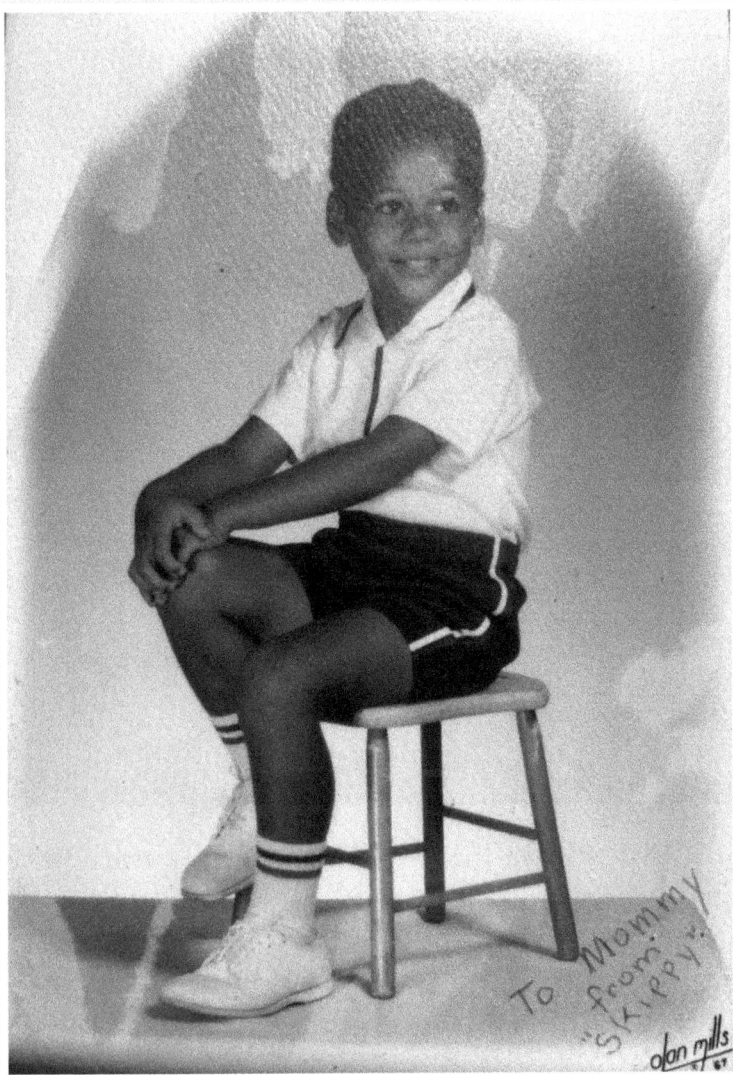

Skip, Age 4

My Brother-in-law Leroy, My Sister Louise, and Skip

Chapter Eight
SECOND TIME AROUND
(1968)

I LOVED STUDENT teaching and had a great supervisor, Mrs. Ethel Perry. She was an excellent teacher and loved her first-grade students. I learned more from her than I had in any class before student teaching. I observed her closely and studied her methods because I wanted to be the kind of teacher she was. I continued to refuse to date the men who asked; however, one of them did not give up. Several times a week, he sent messages to me through a book given by one of his students. The messages, asking me to have a martini with him after work, were written on a napkin. A picture of a martini was on the napkin.

After receiving so many of these messages, Mrs. Perry told me to tell my suitor that I had work to do and no time to read messages from him. She knew who was sending the messages because she recognized the students from his class. He slowed down on sending messages but did not give up pursuing me. His name was James "Jimmy" E. Carter. I completed my student teaching experience with a grade of B in 1967 and moved on to my first teaching position in the fall of 1967. I was driving my little Volkswagen to work every day, living on the little money I was making, and I could not keep up with the car payments. The dealership sent a representative out to repossess the car. My mother told the representative that if he could give me a little time, she would cash in an insurance policy to pay what was owed on the car. The representative agreed, and I was able to keep my car.

When I discovered Jimmy was not single, I told him I would not discuss dating anymore until he could provide documented proof of being single. He believed me and provided original documentation of his single status in May 1967. We dated and got to know each other better. I introduced him to my family and Skip, and they liked him. My mother was not happy because she was skeptical of me being serious with someone who was divorced. He introduced me to his parents, and they accepted me immediately.

We continued to date, and he proposed marriage. I accepted and suggested that instead of a full-blown church wedding, we have a marriage ceremony in his church. He agreed, and we decided on the date of February 10, 1968. I was twenty-five, he was twenty-nine, and Skip was five. We only invited family and close friends. We did not send out invitations but called the invitees and told them not to bring gifts; we only wanted their presence. We did not have a reception. We left immediately for our three-day honeymoon as we both had to return to work. My mother took care of Skip while we were on our honeymoon. They got along like two peas in a pod all the time. Skip was invited to a birthday party the day of the marriage and chose the party over the ceremony. I always let him make his own decisions if they were not major.

Skip and I moved into the house where Jimmy was raised, an old house built in 1901 in a mixed-income neighborhood in downtown Augusta, Georgia. People in the neighborhood liked one another and got along well. I liked the house, but for several reasons I did not want to live there forever. I told Jimmy I would live there for five years, then we would have to move, and he agreed. However, to my surprise, in four years he told me he was ready to build us a house. That was the shock of my life. He told me to look at house plans and find what I wanted. Well, we looked at house plans together and found something we agreed on. We found the property we liked in rural Augusta and built our house.

It was a beautiful house in a lovely neighborhood, the best house I had ever lived in! We lived there for twenty-seven years and decided to downsize and sell when we became empty nesters. We then bought a condominium in downtown Augusta. The building where the condominium was located had twenty-four-hour security, underground parking, a clubroom for entertainment, a small gym/spa room, and other amenities. It was perfect for people of our age. We have lived in this condominium for twenty-five years.

My marriage to Jimmy has not been perfect, but it has been beautiful. It has been free from any physical or mental abuse. He has done his best to take care of me and Skip. We have been married for fifty-six years. He is very considerate of me and has booked a cruise on Royal Caribbean's *Icon of the Seas* so the three of us could celebrate my eighty-second birthday on the ship.

Judy and Jimmy at an AKA Founders Day.
He was the only male in attendance.

Jimmy, skip and me together shortly after
Jimmy and I married in 1968.

This is me at my 80th birthday party.

My mother a few years before she became ill and passed away.

Jimmy's Parents

Jimmy and Judy at their new home.

Jimmy and Judy

The house Jimmy built for us in West Augusta.

*Jimmy, Skip, and me with his parents at an Omega
Psi Phi Fraternity Conference in Florida 1982.*

Jimmy was raised in this house

Chapter Nine

THE BIG DISAPPOINTMENT AND
BEGINNING MY TEACHING CAREER
(1967–1968)

I COMPLETED STUDENT teaching with a B grade in 1967. The Registrar's Office informed me that I needed three credit hours in any subject to graduate. I had already been hired by the Richmond County Board of Education to teach in a predominantly white elementary school, so I was allowed to march in the baccalaureate ceremony but not the graduation ceremony. My mother was so proud that I had graduated college. During the summer of 1967, a Desegregation of Schools Institute was offered to teachers at the Paine College Campus.

I asked the academic dean of the college if I could enroll in the institute. He said I could if the director of the institute approved. I went to the director and explained my situation, and he approved my acceptance into the institute, which granted five credit hours. I completed the program with a grade of P (passing), which all participants received. I went to the registrar and presented the information about having completed the hours I needed to graduate, and I expected to receive my degree. The registrar did not accept the hours, stating that I did not get her approval to take the institute. I told her I had the academic dean's approval, but she would not accept it.

Therefore, I began teaching without a degree and without the full salary of a certified teacher. I went back to school while teaching and took a three-hour course in visual aids. When I completed that course, the registrar granted the degree in elementary education. I lost money because of her selfish decision. The story is that I completed my work for graduation in the summer of 1967, started teaching, but did not receive my degree until the fall of 1968.

As the line from the poem "Mother to Son" states, "Life for me ain't been no crystal stair."

As stated above, I began teaching in the fall of 1967 at Windsor Spring Elementary School. I was assigned to sixth graders, teaching all subjects. I was one of two black teachers in that school. I was overexcited. There were about twenty-four students in my class: twenty-two white and two black. The first evening after school, a white mother called me and asked why I did not go to a "nigger" school. I told her that there was no such thing as a "nigger" school and that I was assigned to that school; I did not ask to go there. I also told her that she could come to the school the next morning and have her son transferred to another teacher. For some reason, she did not come, and her son remained in my class. He was one of my brightest students, and I did not have any trouble from him.

My beginning salary working for the Richmond County Board of Education was $4,270.12 a year (because I did not have my degree) and ended at $8,810.88 a year. Everything went well at Windsor Spring Elementary School until February 1968. My students were eager to learn, and I was eager to teach them. However, in February, I thought Black History Week was supposed to be celebrated. I asked my students to tell me what they knew about the contributions of black people to America. They did not know about contributions, but they had heard the names of Booker T. Washington, George Washington Carver, Harriet Tubman, and recently, Martin Luther King, Jr.

I thought I had to do something about that gap in their learning, so I went to the public library and borrowed some books on black history (on their level). I placed the books on a table in our classroom and asked them to examine the books carefully and select one to read. I also told them to write or visually show what they learned from the book. In a week or so, they presented the results to me. I was amazed by what they presented. There were poems, illustrated poems, stories, and collages.

I asked the librarian to come to my room and see what my students had done. She was so excited she asked if she could display the artifacts in the library's showcase. The students gave their permission. Of course, the students told their parents about their work and the display. Two days later when we arrived at school, the artifacts had been removed from the showcase. I went to the principal and asked what happened. He told me that some parents had called the superintendent and told him they did not want their children to learn about black history and to tell me to stop teaching it. He also said the superintendent told him to destroy the black history artifacts, and he wanted to see me in his office that day after school.

I went to the superintendent's office, and this is what was said: He told me about the phone calls from several parents and how upset they were. He instructed me to teach only what was in the history book and nothing more. I told him that not enough black history was in the history book. He insisted that I accept this and not continue to upset parents. It's important to know that not all parents of children in my class were upset. The superintendent gave me a letter for my records, summarizing what had been discussed. Well, the following year in February, I continued teaching black history. Once again, I was called to the superintendent's office and received the same story and letter. Some of my students told me their parents refused to sign a petition circulating in the neighborhood to stop me from teaching black history to them. I was grateful for that.

My students continued to learn in the traditional, standard way, but we also included nontraditional ways of learning. I was in a master's program learning all kinds of exciting ways to motivate students to learn and be excited about it. I tried some of these methods on my students. Later, you will read about what my students thought in chapter 11.

To make a long story short, I was in this school for five years and received the same letter each year. Terminating me was never mentioned, just a letter telling me to teach what was in the history book. I completed my fifth year at Windsor Spring Elementary School. During that time, we had a wonderful time experiencing new adventures in learning. At the beginning of my sixth year, a new principal was assigned to the school and rearranged the schedule completely. There was an early morning schedule and an evening schedule. He assigned some of us to the evening schedule without conferring with us. I was not interested in teaching in the late evening, so I went to the superintendent to ask for a transfer to another school.

I was transferred to Roy Rollins Elementary School in the fall of 1972, which was located a short distance from my former school. The student composition was about the same, although there were more black teachers at this school. It was still predominantly white with parents of the same mentality as the school I had left. I was assigned to teach sixth and seventh graders.

When I received my homeroom roster, I called every parent on the roster and introduced myself. I also explained my expectations for their children: I did not tolerate misbehavior or disrespect. I further explained that while I was not trained to be a police officer, I was a dynamic teacher who would give my all to ensure the children received the best education possible. I then invited the parents to visit my classroom so we could talk further in person.

In those days, teachers were allowed to spank children with signed permission from parents. I told them I required permission even if the child would never need spanking. I needed this because if a parent did not give permission and the child knew it, they might think they could misbehave, and the teacher could not do anything about it. I said if they couldn't sign the permission slip, they would have to transfer their child to another teacher. To my surprise, none of the children were transferred from my class.

I continued to teach black history during Black History Week but did not get a letter from the Board of Education. It was because the new superintendent's daughter was in my class, and he was not racist. We did a lot of interesting things in the four years I was at Roy Rollins. I taught sixth and seventh grades for three years, and the principal asked if I would consider moving to fifth grade to strengthen the program there. I had to think about it because I had not taught that age group before. I loved teaching sixth and seventh graders and did not think I would like the lower grade, but I decided to try it, and it turned out to be exciting. You will read about what the fifth grade students thought about being in my class in their own words later in chapter 11.

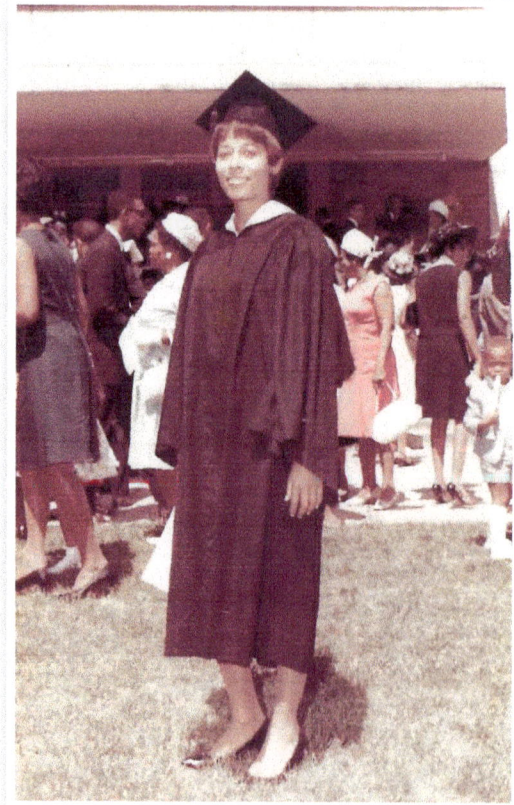

Judy after marching in the ceremony at Paine College.

Chapter Ten
MY TEACHING CAREER IN HIGHER EDUCATION BEGAN—A LONG JOURNEY
(1976–2011)

SOMETHING EXCITING HAPPENED during my fourth year at Rollins. The president of Paine College, Dr. Julius S. Scott Jr., who had come in and changed the ethos of Paine College, called and told me he wanted me to come to Paine and help train students in the education department to become good teachers. He said he had read articles in the local newspaper about me and my students. I immediately expressed that I had never considered teaching at the college level. However, my husband encouraged me to try this new adventure. He thought I might like it. I thought about it for several weeks and decided to accept. Even though I hated leaving my students, I soon learned to love higher education.

This gave me the opportunity to have input into what I thought teacher education should be. Additionally, I had already begun a master's program at Augusta College (now Augusta University) in 1973. I was not interested in graduate study because I thought I was not smart enough, but my husband told me I was smart enough and would do well. He kept encouraging me until I took the plunge.

After applying to Augusta College and being accepted, I took classes in the evenings after school. I never took a leave of absence because I could not afford to financially. I had wonderful professors who made learning interesting, and I was surprised because I thought graduate school would be too difficult to like. My favorite professor was Dr. Geraldine Hargrove, Dean of the College of Education and teacher of advanced reading, who later became an integral part on my doctoral committee at the University of South Carolina in Columbia.

While teaching and going to graduate school, I had major help from my husband, his mother, and my mother. My husband took over additional household duties, and the ladies took turns making dinner for the family at least twice a week (excluding weekends). I had so much support I did not have any excuse for not doing well. I successfully completed the master's degree on June 19, 1976, making better grades than I got in undergraduate school. My mother was super proud of me. This was another milestone for me. I entered the doctoral program in 1978 and graduated in 1981. I received a grant to study from the United Negro College Fund. My mother was ecstatic!

I began teaching at Paine College in the fall of 1976. My starting salary was $10,000. My first position was serving as instructor and director of the student teaching program. I fell in love with this level of teaching. It was amazing to see so many bright students who wanted to become teachers, and I was thrilled to be able to help them fulfill their wishes. Since I had no experience teaching at this level, I had to work hard to learn.

Being in graduate school at this time was a blessing. I studied every move of my exciting professors and emulated as much as possible what they did in my classroom with my students. This worked for us. Not only was I teaching and directing the student teaching program, but I also did other things such as writing grants and recruiting high school students for teacher education, advising and mentoring students who were in the Alpha Kappa Alpha Sorority, Inc., and starting a program in one of the elementary schools to help underachieving boys who were not doing well academically and socially improve. I represented the college in the community in many ways. Evidence of what my students, mentees, administrators, colleagues, and others thought about my instruction and involvement can be read in chapter 11: I loved this job!

In 1981 the Division of Education at the University of South Carolina Aiken asked me to come and serve as associate professor and director of the student teaching program. I was reluctant at first, but the increase in salary of $20,000 was attractive. I accepted and enjoyed the experience. After four years at University of South Carolina Aiken, in 1984 the new president of Paine College, Dr. William Harris, a Paine College graduate, asked me to return to Paine as chair of the Division of Education. I worked with Dr. Harris, and we did remarkable things at Paine until he accepted a position as president of a large university in Texas. Dr. Scott had resigned and accepted another position with the Methodist Church. I accepted a salary of $30,000 a year, and what happened next is explained by Dr. William Harris in chapter 11.

In 1988 Dr. Scott returned as president, and I remained until 1993. At the end of the ninth year, I unfortunately resigned because of a dispute (recommended termination of a colleague who tried to sabotage my program during a Southern Association of Colleges and Schools [SACS] visit) with Dr. Scott who had brought me there in 1976. Dr. Scott's comments regarding my resignation are in chapter 11.

In 1993, about two weeks after I resigned, I received a telephone call from Dr. Samuel DuBois Cook, president of Dillard University in New Orleans, Louisiana, asking me to consider coming to Dillard to chair the Department of Education. I said no for many reasons. He told me he had done a national search and did not find anyone acceptable for the position. He said a friend of his told him to try to get me to come to Dillard. To make a long story short, I accepted after making two trips to the campus to meet administrators and faculty and explore living conditions.

Dr. Cook asked me a question I had never been asked before: "What would it take (salary wise) for you to come to Dillard?" Not knowing what to say and thinking about my current salary ($35,000), I said $60,000. He gave me a contract for what I asked in a few hours. (I wish I had asked for more.) The salary offer was more than I ever expected. I informed Dr. Cook that I could stay at Dillard for five years. (This was what I promised my husband.) I said that because it usually took five years to rebuild a program, including staying around to evaluate progress. I had prayed long and hard before I accepted the position. It was not only an opportunity but also a sacrifice, as I had to relocate to another state.

My husband and I found a gated apartment complex located about five miles from Dillard's campus, and I lived there for five years. This meant we had a "commuter marriage." However, this turned out to be the best career decision ever, and my career exploded because of it. Jimmy and I worked out a plan that made this transition suitable for both of us. I would fly home some weekends, and he would fly to New Orleans some weekends to visit me. On his trips to visit me, we explored New Orleans's music culture, as Jimmy loved jazz.

What my amazing staff and I did at Dillard was recognized by the president, faculty, Board of Education, State Department of Education, community, and national organizations. The students excelled as they had done at Paine, and recruiters sought them out. Before I left Dillard, Dr. Cook had recommended me for tenure, and my salary was $80,000. I not only enjoyed working at Dillard (which had the most beautiful campus ever), but I also loved the people, the culture, the food, and the ambiance of the city. This was the experience of my life. Dr. Cook retired in my fourth year at Dillard, and I worked one more year (my fifth year) and left. Dr. Cook's wife, Sylvia, and I had become good friends, and that friendship still stands today. You will read what Dr. Cook had to say about what happened at Dillard in chapter 11.

My next experience was at Livingstone College in Salisbury, North Carolina. In 1998 Dr. Burnette Joiner, with whom I had worked at Dillard University, asked if I would come there to help. He was a new president at Livingstone and needed some new persons to assist him in making significant changes. He created a position for me as associate vice president of academic services with a salary of $80,000). He also hired a person to serve as director of student affairs and a person to chair the assessment component of the SACS review coming up. Our salaries were the same.

I had to relocate again, as Livingstone was a four-hour drive from Augusta. I lived in an apartment in a beautiful house located on campus. I could have walked to my office, but I did not. I enjoyed my work at Livingstone, but during the third year, the president was suddenly terminated for some unforeseen reason. The interim president called in me and the two other women whom Dr. Joiner had hired and told us we had to cut our salaries because he could not balance the budget with what we were making. I responded by cutting my salary by 25 percent. However, he responded that my recommended cut was not enough. Consequently, I resigned and left Livingstone because I was not about to work for nothing. I sent Dr. Aymer a letter explaining why I left, and he responded that I had misinterpreted why he wanted to balance the budget. The two other women left also. A letter to document that exchange can be read in chapter 11. Dr. Joiner's comments are also in chapter 11. About a week after my resignation, in 2001, the president of Voorhees College in Denmark, South Carolina, Dr. Leonard Dawson, asked me to come there to serve as associate vice president of academic affairs. He said he knew he could not offer the salary I was accustomed to and offered a salary of $55,000. I accepted because he needed my help. I also accepted because he was a friend of my husband, and the college was close enough for a daily commute. My duties included being responsible for the overall administration of the academic program of the college and rebuilding the teacher education program.

Dr. Dawson retired two years after he hired me, and a new president was hired. He promoted me to vice president of academic affairs. It was not long, about a year, when I discovered we did not share the same philosophy on quality education or agree on many issues related to improving academic affairs. The faculty and I made many changes to the curriculum, and enrollment increased. I included the faculty in all major decisions. They respected me, and I respected them. However, Because of my disagreements with some of the president's proposals and other issues, he eventually offered me a demotion from vice president of academic affairs to distinguished professor of education with the same salary. (I had already been recognized as distinguished professor at Paine College.)

Therefore, I refused his offer and resigned the same day. I told him it was a demotion, and he said it was not because I was getting the same salary. The same salary with a different title was a demotion as far as I was concerned. I told him that money was not the most important factor in my life, and I was not ever going to sacrifice my values and principles for money. I found out that day, before I left the campus, the president had introduced my replacement in a faculty meeting. He told the faculty members he had offered me another position, and I was thinking about it (not that I refused). The faculty members were horrified. It is interesting to note that my replacement was a friend of this president and had recently been terminated from a college in Mississippi. You will read more about what I did at Voorhees and what happened after I left in chapter 11. After I left Voorhees in July 2003, I was home for about three weeks when the dean of the School of Education at Benedict College in Columbia, who was also a friend, called and asked if I would come there to help. She heard I had left Voorhees College. After two years there, I was named chair of the Department of Education. I encountered the most interesting students I will never forget. Because Columbia was a two-hour drive from Augusta, I decided to rent an apartment, stay in Columbia during the week, and go home on weekends. Again, I enjoyed my work here, and another great offer was made.

In 2006, my former president at Paine College, Dr. William Harris, who was now interim president of Fort Valley State University, called and told me he wanted me to come there to serve as dean of the School of Education. What can I say? I accepted this offer because this was the highest position I had ever been offered, not to mention the salary was $105,000 (at a state institution). For many years, Fort Valley State University had one of the best reputations for graduating first-rate teachers in Georgia. However, after many years of operation, it lost its accreditation. Because Fort Valley was a two-and-a-half-hour drive from Augusta, I had to relocate. My husband and I found a lovely apartment in a gated community that was close to the campus. I worked during the week and went home on weekends. There were several times when I could not go home on weekends because of the work that had to be done.

My job there was challenging. I had never had to rebuild a program that had lost all accreditation. That meant we had to start from nothing as if the program never existed. After reviewing what was needed, we began working. I had inherited an amazing group of professionals who were already in the School of Education. However, I soon discovered there were some professors in the group who did not want to do what was required to rebuild the program. I recommended termination of these people to the new president, Dr. Larry Rivers, a graduate of Fort Valley State University. Dr. Rivers had been extremely supportive of the College of Education since his arrival. With the documentation I provided, Dr. Rivers terminated the professors I recommended.

After this, faculty members who had initially worked hard joined me in getting the job done. We worked long days and some nights for months to rebuild the program and gain reaccreditation. After submitting appropriate documentation, we were finally granted a visit from the Professional Standards Commission, a government entity responsible for certifying Georgia colleges and universities for accreditation. This visit was successful. Now we had to prepare for a visit from the Southern Association of Colleges and Schools (SACS). SACS is an educational accreditor recognized by the United States Department of Education and the Council for Higher Education Accreditation. With no time to rest, we continued the arduous task of preparing for SACS. The day and night work became longer, as we sometimes left the building at 2:00 or 3:00 a.m. We also worked on weekends.

Months later, we submitted the appropriate documentation to SACS. After SACS officials reviewed the documentation, we were granted a visit. The visiting team of professionals was on our campus for almost a week, examining every piece of evidence, going through records of faculty credentials and financial records, and interviewing students, faculty, administrators, public school personnel, and anyone else they wanted to. We met all requirements and were approved for reaccreditation by SACS. This was the most wonderful achievement for us in the College of Education as well as the university. President Rivers was ecstatic! You will read what he thought, as well as others in chapter 11.

Some of the key players in success of this achievement were Drs. Eleanor Sikes, Jean Waycaster, Julius Scipio, Violet Johnson, Alfreda Manson, Gregory Green, Jerry Mobley, Teah Moore, Curtis Borne, and Tom Jarvis. Two other important contributors were President Larry Eugene Rivers and my administrative assistant, Ms. Clara Tarver.

I completed my five-year commitment to Fort Valley State University in 2011. I finally retired from full-time work. The university gave me a going-away banquet fit for a queen. My staff, other faculty, administrators, and my family and friends from Augusta and South Carolina were present. We had a great time, an event I will never forget.

I came home to rest and enjoy my retirement when I got a call from the new president's wife at Paine College, telling me she needed my help. The Department of Education was preparing for a reaccreditation visit from the Georgia Professional Standards Commission (GaPSC). Naturally, I told her I would come and help for a year, and that year lasted three years. I did not negotiate a salary because Paine College is my alma mater. I knew the college was in financial trouble and accepted the token they could afford for my services. I had been so blessed by God; there was no need not to do what is required by him: to whom much is given, much is required.

I worked with the faculty in the Department of Education and the president's wife, who is an outstanding educator, for three years, reviewing the requirements for GaPSC accreditation. They had already made a decent start. The main problem was some faculty members, as well as the chair of the department, were not familiar with the requirements. Once everyone understood the requirements, we made progress. We worked hard day and night to correct the deficiencies. There were some hurt feelings and words said that caused negative attitudes. However, the work had to go on. Eventually, we came to understand one another, and the work was easier. To make a long story short, we presented the required documentation to GaPSC and were granted a visit. A team of professionals visited the campus for several days to review documents, search through files, and interview persons in different areas on campus and public school personnel. After a thorough review, the Department of Education was reaccredited by GaPSC.

I went home again thinking I was not going to work again. What happened? A friend of mine, Dr. Paula Dehoney, the associate dean of the College of Education at Augusta University, called and told me the Department of Education needed a chair and asked if I would be interested. I told her I was not interested in assuming a position like that again, but I would come for a year to keep things in order and help them find a suitable person for the position. After my conversation with Dr. Dehoney, the new dean of the College of Education, Dr. Zack Kellaher, arrived. He reviewed my credentials and informally interviewed me. He told me he was pleased to have me on board. We worked together beautifully, and he often complimented my work and professionalism.

Toward the end of the year, Dr. Kellaher asked if I would stay another year. Of course, I said I could not because of a promise I had made to my husband. I enjoyed the time spent at Augusta University. I became connected with students, faculty, and staff. I visited professors' classrooms and evaluated their teaching strategies. I visited student teachers in public schools and evaluated them. I held monthly meetings with faculty and discussed getting prepared for a SACS review. I enjoyed the time spent at Augusta University, and I never imagined when I was a student in the master's program that someday I would be working there as interim chair of the Department of Education and professor. Dr. Dehoney's comments are in chapter 11.

That was my last job working full-time. I am now enjoying retirement, organizations, church ministry, and helping others whenever I can. My life is full, and I enjoy every minute of it. The sacrifices I made to accept positions out of town were made because God told me to go to these different institutions because they needed my help. He told me I had to share the abilities he provided me and not be selfish and keep them to myself. I kept hearing, "To whom much is given, much is required."

"Before I formed you in the womb, I knew you. Before you were born, I set you apart; I appointed you as a prophet to the nations'. (Jeremiah 1:5).

There is an old Negro spiritual song that reminds me of my life and journey. The lyrics read,

Lord, I've done what you told me to do,
For your love is going to carry me through,
I've had troubles all my life, many times I had to
sacrifice, but I won't give up, I'm staying strong, 'cause I
know the Lord will help me carry on.
Through the years I felt it hard to go on, but I know the
Lord will help me carry on.
Lord, I've done what you told me to do
For your love is going to carry me through,
I pray to you, Lord, that you send blessings my way, so
that I may go at least another day,
But I won't give up, I'm staying strong, 'cause I know
that the Lord will carry me on.
Lord, I've done what you told me to do
For your love is going to carry me through.

The day I received the doctorate degree.

Employers Reflections

University of South Carolina
At Aiken
171 University Parkway
Aiken, South Carolina 29801

Chancellor
(803) 648-6851

August 14, 1981

Dr. Judy Carter
1528 Flagler Road
Augusta, Georgia 30909

Dear Dr. Carter:

I am pleased to offer you a Tenure-Track appointment to the faculty of the University of South Carolina at Aiken at the rank of Assistant Professor. If you accept, the appointment will be effective August 16, 1981. Your duties for the academic year will have been fulfilled when you have submitted all final grades for courses taught during the Spring Semester 1982. The salary for the 1981-82 academic year will be $20,000. Your duties include directing the student teaching program, directing the field placement program, teaching the equivalent of six hours per semester and other duties as assigned by Dr. Gaston Bloodsworth, Chairperson—Division of Education. You will be expected to schedule regular office hours and to advise students as part of your duties. Additionally you will be eligible to participate in all fringe benefits available to University employees. Taxes, social security, and retirement payments will be deducted from your paychecks as appropriate.

If you find these terms acceptable, please sign one copy of this offer below and return it to me. The other copy is for your files. We are delighted that you will be joining our faculty for the coming year and expect you to make a significant contribution.

Sincerely,
William C. Casper
Chancellor

I accept the contract and terms as specified above.

William H. Harris
6 Oyster Landing Road
Hilton Head Island, SC 29928
(843) 671-5832

3 August 2003

Dr. Judy Carter has informed me of her intention to change jobs and has asked me to write in support of her effort to relocate. Accordingly, I gladly write this letter for the file and for her use and I would be most pleased to speak further with anyone who wishes further confirmation of my commendation of this fine teacher/scholar.

I first came to know Dr. Carter as a professional educator when she worked with me as Chairman of the Division of Education and Director of Teacher Education when I was President of Paine College during the early and mid-1980s. Under Dr. Carter's leadership we completely revamped and improved the teacher education program at the college and heightened significantly the performance of our teacher graduates on state teacher examinations and in the classrooms of the school systems in which they won appointments. Indeed, Dr. Carter's work gained her high recognition from leading teacher education leaders of the State of Georgia, recognition that resulted in significant appointments on commissions and committees concerned about improving teacher education and the quality of teachers throughout the State of Georgia.

Dr. Carter's career took her to positions at Dillard University in New Orleans where I remained familiar with her work, and on to the University of South Carolina at Aiken and to Voorhees College. Through these moves she took on higher and higher responsibilities in higher education leadership. Combined, these successful experiences have primed Dr. Carter for additional contributions to higher education. She is a skilled and dedicated educator and would be a fine addition to your organization. I recommend her enthusiastically and without reservation.

Sincere Best Wishes,
William H. Harris

Mrs. Judy Carter
1528 Flagler Road
Augusta, Georgia 30909

Dear Mrs. Carter:

Your request for release from your 1981 contract was received. I regret the decision to terminate your excellent and competent services to Paine College, but understand the circumstances. You are released from the contract.

Regrettably, some of the funds made available to you for study were from the United Negro College Fund. There is a stipulation that recipients of these funds must return to the employing institution, transfer to another UNCF member college, or replace the funds. I am requesting the Business Manger to prepare a statement of UNCF funds you received.

You have rendered loyal and effective service to Paine College, and you will be missed by many, especially students, who have consistently evaluated you highly. I had come to depend on your for so many things, all of which you did so well, that I don't look forward to the new academic year with joy. But I hope you will enjoy the new challenges and responsibilities which you now face, and wish you the best of luck.

Sincerely yours,

Julius S. Scott, Jr.

Samuel DuBois Cook, Ph.D., LL.D., L.H.D.
3360 Laren Lane, S.W.
Atlanta, Georgia 30311

President Emeritus
Dillard University

August 1, 2003

To Whom It May Concern

Reference: Dr. Judy L. Carter

For a number of compelling reasons, I am honored, privileged, and delighted to recommend Dr. Judy L. Carter for a major administrative, faculty, or staff position in higher education.

First, Dr. Carter has a well-earned national reputation in higher education. She has a passion for academic excellence and has been deeply involved, as a teacher, scholar, administrator, mentor, and public intellectual in higher education since 1975. She is first-rate. During my long tenure as President of Dillard University, we had the wonderfully fortunate experience, after a national search, to recruit Dr. Carter as Chair of the Division of Education. She did a remarkable job. Graduates of her division had a peerless record of success on the NTE (National Teacher's Examination)—a striking improvement over the past.

Second, Dr. Carter is energetic, hard-working, enthusiastic, articulate, and imaginative as a faculty member and administrator. She is so committed to her responsibilities that she will work nights, week-ends, and holidays to get the job done. Her commitment is overwhelming.

Third, Dr. Carter is vigorously committed to high ideals and noble goals of striving. She is a consensus-builder, a magnificent colleague, a superb fund-raiser, an inspiring leader, a wise mentor, and excellent role model.

Fourth, Dr. Carter is a person of the highest personal and professional standards. She embodies integrity, character, honor, vision, commitment, and decency. She will be a genuine asset to any college or university in the country.

I recommend Dr. Judy L. Carter with immense confidence and great enthusiasm.

All good wishes,

Sincerely yours,
Samuel DuBois Cook

Bell Law Firm
1111 14th Street, N.W.
Suite 777
Washington, D.C. 20005
(202) 842-4066
Facsimile (202) 842-0320
March 22, 2007

Personal and Confidential

Dr. Samuel DuBois Cook
3360 Laren Lane, S.W.
Atlanta, Georgia 30311

Re: Presidency of Paine College

Dear Dr. Cook:

This is to thank you for your nomination of Dr. Judy L. Carter for the position of President of Paine College.

Trustee Eddie R. Cheeks, M.D. is the Chair of the Presidential Search Committee. Accordingly, I am forwarding your nomination of Dr. Carter to Dr. Cheeks and his committee in order that she may be fully considered by the Presidential Search Committee. You and Dr. Carter should be hearing from Dr. Cheeks and the search committee shortly regarding your nomination, her candidacy and the time frame in which all applications and nominations will be reviewed.

The College and the Board extend our thanks to you for your willingness to help us identify and consider candidates for the presidency of Paine College.

Very truly yours,
Robert L. Bell, Chair
Paine College Board of Trustees

RLB/vg
cc: Dr. Eddie R. Cheeks (w/enclosure)
Chair, Presidential Search Committee
Paine College
1235 Fifteenth Street
Augusta, Georgia 30901

State of South Carolina
Department of Education
Inez Moore Tenenbaum
State Superintendent of Education

June 10, 2003

Dr. Judy Carter
Vice President of Academic Affairs
Voorhees College
1411 Voorhees Road
Denmark, South Carolina 29042

Dear Dr. Carter:

On June 6, 2003, the Professional Review Committee (PRC) voted to recommend to the State Board of Education that the teacher education program at Voorhees College should receive the accreditation decision of **Provisional Accreditation (with a focused visit)**. I have enclosed a copy of a summary of the PRC findings.

The recommendation of **Provisional Accreditation (with a focused visit)** will now be presented to the Teacher Recruitment, Training and Certification Committee (TRTC) of the State Board of Education on July 8, 2003. This meeting will be held in the Basement Conference Room of the Rutledge Building.

You and others from your institution may attend the TRTC meeting and present any information that you feel that the State Board of Education should consider in regards to the PRC's recommendation.

Thank you for your efforts to develop a quality teacher preparation program at your institution. If you have questions about this process, please contact me or Jane Turner prior to July 8, 2003. I will notify you of the full State Board of Education action with respect to your teacher preparation program after the scheduled meeting on July 9, 2003.

Sincerely,
Jeffrey R. Wilson. Ed.D.
Office of Teacher Education

State of South Carolina
Department of Education
Inez Moore Tenenbaum
State Superintendent of Education

August 8, 2003

To Whom It May Concern:

I have known **Dr. Judy L. Carter** for about three years. The first time I met Judy, I knew that she was an outstanding educator and a top notch administrator. Judy immediately impressed me with her enthusiasm, love for education, loyalty, and dedication to her new assignment as chairperson of the Education Department of Voorhees College. Judy accepted the challenge of setting about to reestablish the education program at the college. As Co-director of the then South Carolina Title II Teacher Quality Grant, I immediately recognized the confidence and abilities that Judy exuded. Although the college was not a part of the original thirty accredited institutions that could apply for the grant, I allowed Judy to write a sub grant to review the standards and curriculum of Voorhees College and see how the curriculum could be changed to ensure that the college could regain its accreditation. In fact, the stage was set for the reinstatement of the Education Department's accreditation when there was a change of staff. Because Judy was no longer at the helm, the accreditation did not progress as it should have. I developed a bond with Judy and have enjoyed our continued working relationship even though we both have gone on to other things in the educational arena.

Judy has a well earned and well deserved local and national reputation. Judy has shown superb leadership and dedication in making whatever she has been involved in a success. The Standards and Assessment grant that Judy received through the Title II office was handled efficiently and with great care to detail. I would have to say that Judy is without a doubt highly motivated and a worker bee.

I have had many opportunities to see Judy at work with the students of Voorhees and at statewide meetings. She has been a dedicated and meticulous leader. Judy is intelligent and very determined. Her work and perseverance is exceptional. Judy represents herself and the institution where she works in a very positive and professional manner. She continues to amaze me with her wit, professionalism, enthusiasm, and joy.

I highly recommend Dr. Judy Carter as an educational leader in any institution of higher education. She will be a credit to the college, the state, and the nation.

Sincerely,
Barbara Flemming Weston
Co-Director No Child Left Behind
Office of Title II
Division of Teacher Quality

Dr. Judy Carter:
The Indispensable Leader
By
Larry E. Rivers, D.A., Ph.D.
The Eighth President of The Fort Valley State University

In early 2006, The Fort Valley State University (FVSU) an Historically Black College/University founded in 1895, needed a visionary educator to develop and lead a new College of Education (COE). The previous COE had, a year prior, become part of the College of Arts and Sciences (CAS). This exponentially larger CAS was unwieldly, and ultimately untenable structure. Upon my arrival on March 14,2006, I concurred with a plan to separate the former COE from the CAS, I had the utmost confidence in the individual who had been hired about ten weeks earlier, on January 3,2006, to serve as dean of the soon to-be reconstituted FVSU College of Education: Dr. Judy Carter.

Having earned a reputation as an effective administrator, Dr. Carter came to the university well-credentialed. She held a bachelor's degree in Elementary Education from Paine College, a Master of Education degree in Elementary Education from Augusta College (now Augusta University), and a Doctor of Education degree from the University of South Carolina. Dr. Carter continued her post-graduate studies beyond the doctorate degree at Bryn Mawr College and the Harvard University Institute for Higher Education. She became a certified assessor of teacher effectiveness in Georgia, South Carolina, and Louisiana. Prior to coming to FVSU, Dr. Carter served in leading positions at Benedict College, Voorhees College, Livingstone College, Paine College, and Dillard University. Accordingly, I knew that FVSU had selected an experienced executive who could lead the university's College of Education into the future.

Upon her arrival to the campus, Dr. Carter worked tirelessly with the administration, faculty, and student body to reformulate a stand-a lone College of Education. No one at the university had a stronger work ethic than her. Dr. Cater knew exactly what she had to do. Her primary goal focused on securing regional and national accreditation for the COE. She, in cooperation with her faculty, colleagues, staff, and students, accomplished this monumental goal less than two years after her arrival at the university. The college's enrollment continued to grow under her leadership, as well.

Throughout her deanship from January 2, 2006, to June 30, 2011, Dr. Carter demonstrated that she was a hardworking, honest, and no-nonsense administrator. She had a deep commitment to preparing the very best future teachers and scholars. This conviction manifested itself every day in the way in which she served students, supported faculty members, and strove to build a COE that could endure for subsequent generations long after her tenure at FVSU.

Dr. Carter will go down in the annuals of Fort Valley State University history as one of the most outstanding and visionary education deans to ever grace the campus. She leaves a legacy at the COE of Georgia's land -grant historically black university that still stands strong.

Respectfully submitted,
Larry Eugene Rivers, Ph.D. (2024)

Fort Valley State University
A State and Land-Grant University
University System of Georgia
Office of the President
1005 State University Drive • Fort Valley, Georgia 31030-4313

March 27, 2007

Attorney Robert Bell
1111 14th Street NW
Washington, DC 20005

Dear Attorney Bell:

It is with great pleasure and honor that I nominate and strongly recommend to you and the search committee, as well as the university community, Dr. Judy Carter, Dean of the College of Education at the Fort Valley State University, for the position of President of Paine College. Not often is a colleague granted the opportunity to recommend an outstanding scholar and academician to serve in the primary leadership position at one of the finest institutions in our state. While it is an honor, I also feel compelled to introduce to the search committee a prolific and nationally recognized leader in higher education, and administrator, that certainly has the skills and experience to successfully lead the college at this time.

Dr. Carter is currently serving as Dean of the College of Education at the Fort Valley State University where she has been instrumental in developing new and innovative academic programs, improving and enhancing the facilities and infrastructure, actively increasing and advancing fund raising efforts and sponsored programs in the college, increasing enrollment and rebuilding a first class and nationally recognized education program and college. In addition, she has been exceptionally effective at resolving countless issues and working with an aggressive Professional Standards Committee for the State of Georgia and NCATE.

She has exemplified strong leadership, motivation, enthusiasm and tenacity, and with over three decades of experience in higher education she is uniquely qualified to lead Paine College, or any university in the nation. She has a variety of experiences in administration, accreditation efforts, institutional effectiveness, enrollment management, research and sponsored programs, advancement and development, technology, fiscal management and infrastructure development. Coupled with these experiences, Dr. Carter has continued membership and service in various community based, religious, social, civic, professional and academic related organizations.

It is obvious that Dr. Carter is well prepared to lead this prestigious institution, having served as Dean and Vice-President at several colleges and universities. Her preparation and service has been a testament to her commitment to academic excellence. Obviously, these experiences, along with being a successful sitting Dean, have prepared her for the next role of leadership. With an unyielding confidence, again, I nominate and highly recommend Dr. Judy Carter, for the position of President of Paine College. Her contact information is as follows: 1005 State University Drive; Hubbard Building, College of Education; Fort Valley State University; Fort Valley, GA, 31030; (478)825-6366. If I can provide any additional information, please do not hesitate to contact me.

Sincerely,
Larry E. Rivers, D.A., Ph.D.
President

Elementary Students Reflections

My Reflection:

Mrs. Carter was my 6th grade teacher in 1969 at Windsor Spring Elementary School. What I recall about her as a teacher was that she wanted to engage her students and she would enthusiastically do this in all sorts of ways. I was asked, along with a fellow student, to participate in a summer writing camp at Paine College in Augusta by Mrs. Carter. I am so glad I participated as we learned a lot about creative writing & poetry. I clearly remember discovering & writing Haiku poetry & limericks. I also recall that Mrs. Carter asked each student to keep a literature notebook for the year with some of our writings, drawings, etc. I kept that notebook for over 30 years, occasionally taking it out & looking at it, which always brought joy.

Additionally, I recall that we learned about black history during the school year. I had never heard or learned anything about Martin Luther King, Rosa Parks or Langston Hughes. I found their stories fascinating. After recently finding out that Mrs. Carter was reprimanded about teaching black history in 1969 & onward, this illuminates some of her character. She was a trailblazer and risk taker because she wanted to engage & really help students grow & mature. I am indeed grateful that I had Mrs. Carter as a teacher & that she affected in a very positive way, who I became. I am sure this holds true for many other students over her long career. Thank you for all of your hard work & dedication, Mrs. Carter!

I graduated high school in the Augusta area. I then attended Augusta College & earned a bachelor's of science degree. I worked in medical research for 10 years at the Medical College of Georgia. I then homeschooled my daughter through high school After she left for college, I was a bakery director at a local bakery in Augusta for 2 years & then finished out my career as an administrative assistant.

I am married, have 2 children & currently live in Utah, where my husband & I like to travel, hike, bike, go exploring in a Jeep, kayak & paddleboard.

Kim Fender (2024)

Tribute

Judy Carter <judycarter198@hotmail.com>
Thu 2/8/2024 1:56 PM
To: Judy Carter <judycarter198@hotmail.com>

It is my pleasure to write something about my 6th grade teacher at Windsor Spring Elementary School in 1967-68. It was her first teaching experience, and I was in her class. She was the most incredible teacher ever! She taught me so much! Her magical knowledge of wisdom enlightened me. She was the most beautiful teacher I ever had. She taught me the ethic wisdom of English and Poetry! I was one of her chosen students who had the opportunity to attend an English class at Paine College in Augusta, while in the 6th grade at Windsor Spring Elementary School. I felt honored, grateful and proud to benefit from this Golden Opportunity. My mother adored Mrs. Carter and was happy I was in her class. They became friends and communicated over the years.

Mrs. Carter also worked with the cheerleaders after school several times a week and I was a cheerleader. She was very energetic and helped us a lot. Thank you graciously for being an amazing inspiration in my life. I love you and will be forever humbled by your love and knowledge! Where Thought Goes, Energy Flows… When the Student is ready… The Teacher Appears… Many Blessings on Your Amazing Future, Mrs. Judy Carter.

With Much Love,
Joan Lamb
Master Cosmetologist in Augusta, GA. (2024)

Reflections of Mrs. Judy Carter:

My 5th grade teacher at Roy E. Rollins Elementary in Augusta, Georgia for the 1975-1976 school year.

In the summer of 1975, our family moved across the Savannah River from Aiken, South Carolina to Augusta, Georgia. While it was only a 25-mile move, it might as well have been across the country. Augusta was a much larger city. Further, I had been in a private school in Aiken from K-3rd grade, and in a public school for 4th grade. (In the Aiken of 1975, there was not much of a difference in the demographics of my private school and my 4th public school class.) Augusta was much different. The school population was much more diverse, and, going into 5th grade, I had my first African American teacher. Desegregation in Augusta was in effect and children were bussed into Roy E. Rollins from all over Augusta. It was a time of massive change, and racial tensions were high.

I distinctly remember walking to school with my neighborhood friends that first day of 5th grade and sitting down at my desk. The woman in the front reminded me of movie star Diahann Carroll and was one of the best dressed women I had ever seen in what looked to me to be a very expensive pantsuit. She spoke and introduced herself as Mrs. Carter with perfect diction. I thought to myself, "I want to be just like her!" I only knew Mrs. Carter for one year and that year was one of the most impactful years which shaped my views on equality, hard work, and experiential learning opportunities.

As Executive Director of an inner-city nonprofit on the westside of Chicago, I have put into practice many of the lessons I learned from Mrs. Carter. For example, in 1976 many people, especially children, had never flown in a plane, so Mrs. Carter made it possible to fly the ENTIRE 5th grade for a field trip. We had a day of training in what to expect, and after we all boarded, the pilots and flight attendants helped to calm fears by again telling us what to expect. As we took off, the eyes of everyone were out the windows and looking down at the world below as the pilot told us what we were viewing the entire trip. The impact of this cannot be exaggerated—the world grew larger for ALL the children that day. I have put this into practice by incorporating travel within the city and outside the city for the youth and their families in our programming. Chicago has a beautiful lakefront, but so many on the westside have never seen Lake Michigan in person, walked the lakefront or been in a skyscraper. When a child only sees poverty and disinvestment, their view of the world is diminished. Because of this experience with Mrs. Carter in 5th grade, we try to make sure the youth in our programming have access to and experience with the world outside the blocks in which they live.

Another lesson I learned from Mrs. Carter was to speak clearly and with perfect diction. She expected all the children to carry themselves well by standing tall and with pride. We were not allowed to slouch, speak any slang, or say "ain't" in her classroom. She taught us to have good manners during lunch and to always treat each other with dignity and respect. At the time, I did not fully understand the implications of this, but I saw later in life that good manners and proper speaking allow presence and confidence in any room or any table. The youth we serve on the westside are encouraged to do the same and over the years, we have seen the confidence this grows translating into better job, high school, and college interviews.

Mrs. Carter was also so in tune with each of her students. Although she had a large class, she was able to find gifts and abilities in each student and somehow find time to allow them to grow in those abilities. This lesson was solely responsible for the idea of a group of westside youth starting a company of student-designed wrapping paper to sell to raise funds for their field trips. Watching and experiencing Mrs. Carter develop creative ways to help her students flourish in their gifting is why this could ever have happened.

My views on honoring every person and treating them with dignity was solidified in Mrs. Carter's 5th grade class. I am forever grateful to have had parents that taught me "people are people" and that the differences in skin color were what the Good Lord had created and had called "good." I knew in my head this to be truth, but in Mrs. Carter's 5th grade class we LIVED this truth in every way.

I lost track of Mrs. Carter after my 5th grade year, not knowing what had happened to her. I had thought of her often, when home-schooling my own children for a few years and especially when planning programming for the nonprofit. A couple of years ago, we were able to re-connect and I was finally able to tell her the impact she had on my life, but more importantly, the impact she had on the hundreds of children her influence has touched. I can honestly say she very powerfully and positively impacted not only my 5th grade year, but my entire life, the lives of my children, and hundreds of children on the west and south sides of Chicago.

With much love,
Stephanie Marquardt (2024)
Executive Director, City of Refuge, Chicago, IL.

Dr. Judy Carter was a master at teaching at both the elementary school level and college level respectively. Her ability to approach students with excitement and clarity were of great importance. Her desire for her students to grow cognitively and socially was profound.

In her fifth-grade class, where my daughter had the privilege to be assigned, Judy, my college classmate and friend, exemplified vision and innovation. For example, after completing a science unit on transportation, she introduced her students to two methods of travel that exceeded their experiences. One was an airplane ride to Columbia, South Carolina, to visit the Riverbanks Zoo. They arrived at the airport and were surprised by a reception in their honor. This was arranged by Delta Airlines. Each student was given a flight bag (small) and some other token. After enjoying punch and cookies, the students were transported to the zoo by the parents who met them at the airport in their cars, vans or campers. They spent the day at the zoo and returned home to Augusta, GA., excited and tired.

Another activity to further engage her students was a bus trip to Williamsburg, Virginia. After studying a unit on Colonial Life in the 18th century, she wanted her students to see what Colonial Life looked like. The students saw how the people dressed, what their homes looked like, what their cooking utensils looked like, how they cooked, and what kind of transportation they used to get around. They spent the day in the village exploring everything they could. This trip gave Them an opportunity to compare this village to their hometown. Another fifth-grade teacher and her class went on this trip because Judy's class was not large enough to fill the bus. They did not take any chaperones, just the two teachers and students.

At Paine College, while serving as Chairperson of the Department of Education, Judy used best practices to prepare students for a teaching career. Former students often brag about school systems that searched for them as opposed to them having to laboriously apply for positions in their school systems.

To me, these descriptions of Judy Carter encapsulate the meaning of "Teacher Extraordinaire."

Submitted by,
Betty Tutt
Retired Principal (2024)

College Students Reflections

It is an honor that I am allowed to share what a REMARKABLE WOMAN, Dr. Judy Carter is and the ENORMOUS impact that she made in my life. Dr. Carter was the Chair of the Teacher Education Department at Paine College and the driving force behind producing educators who were prepared to teach on any level. There are many stories, memories, and lessons that I could share about her, but I will briefly share the most impactful ones. I have often read that you are a product of your environment. I did not know what that meant then, but I do understand it fully, now.

I attended Paine College during the years 1988 through 1993. Knowing that My father was a graduate of Paine and encouraged me to attend because of their education program, I applied and was accepted. I was blessed to receive a full athletic scholarship to play volleyball, basketball, track, and field. Paine was one of the best institutions for producing good teachers and had a great reputation for ensuring that all education majors would graduate fully certified, ready to begin working after graduation. You see, at Paine College, if you did not pass the TCT (Teacher Certification Exam), you could not student teach. Many of my peers were offered jobs while they were students teaching. That foundation was set, enforced, and there were no exceptions.

Dr. Carter taught us our Foundation courses and our Education Methods course. She stressed that we must be on time, not miss any classes, know our content, and dress presentable. While this may sound like this is minute, as a student-athlete, meeting these expectations could be challenging. Several of my teammates were in the program to be teachers. We had basketball practice daily at 5 a.m. and again at 4 p.m. On away games, it took a lot of effort to go from a baseball cap, sweats, and basketball shoes to making our hair presentable, putting on a dress or slacks, and putting on hosiery. To Dr. Carter, there were no exceptions. We tried our luck once it backfired. We were returning from a 4-day road trip to play colleges in Alabama, and we returned to campus 45 minutes before her class. That day, we were to be dressed up because we were going to visit some schools. We were so tired, so we decided to tell her that we did not make it back in time to make it to class. The look on her face was scary when she told us that we would have to repeat the course and our grades would go from the grade of A to a D. Our courses were offered every other semester, meaning we had to wait until the following fall semester to retake the course. Some of my peers changed their major, but two of my friends and I decided to take our punishment and push forward. We learned that things would come up and it is not always going to be easy, but we must push through and hold ourselves accountable so that we can do the same for our future students. To remain on track for graduation, I enrolled at Clemson University that summer because I was determined to get through the program and graduate.

Once admitted into the Teacher Education Program, things went well. We always had to turn in our assignments before road trips because it was unacceptable to turn in work late. I would also like to add that Dr. Carter's expectations were consistent throughout the department. Our other professors were amazing as well. We learned a lot and had field experiences to supplement the coursework. In the Spring of 1993, we received our student teaching assignments. My assigned school was East Augusta Middle School. Boy, did I have my hands full. My mentor teacher was Mr. Bynum and he helped me turn all the challenges into teachable moments and I must say that I enjoyed that experience. My overall grade for student teaching was an A.

I can go on and on about my PRICELESS experiences as one of her students and Paine College. I will forever be grateful. Since graduation, I had the honor of working with an evaluation team at Paine to revamp the education program and prepare it for reaccreditation. All were great experiences. So indeed, the lessons learned that will be with me forever are: Be Responsible, Be Accountable and Mediocrity is NOT an Option!

After graduating from Paine College in 1993, I enrolled In Clemson University where I earned an M.Ed. in Counseling. Shortly after, I got married and got my first job teaching Physical Education at Spirit

Creek Middle School in Augusta, Georgia. It was not long before my desire to help more led me to obtain a position as an elementary counselor who served Lamar and John Milledge Elementary schools. After two years, I was offered a position as the senior counselor at Lucy Craft Laney HS. This position paved the way for me to be hired to open the new high school, Cross Creek HS during the 1999-2000 school term. I graduated the first three classes. Soon after that, I earned my ED. S. in Leadership, which opened the door for me to be promoted to an assistant principal position. In 2010, I became the principal of Diamond Lakes Elementary. After seven years, I was assigned to Tobacco Road Elementary where my tenure lasted 5 years before being promoted to principal of T.W. Josey High School for two years. Currently, I am the PBIS/School Culture Administrator at Richmond County Board of Education. It has truly been a BLESSING that I have had the opportunities to work on all levels, which has allowed me to see the rewards of my hard work.

Thank you, Dr. Judy Carter for helping to mold me into the person/educator that I am today! I am forever grateful!

I love you SINCERELY,
NyleecheGreen-McRea

It is with great pleasure and deep gratitude that I pen this foreword for someone whose influence has played an instrumental role in shaping not only my educational philosophy but also the trajectory of my professional journey. Driven by a relentless commitment to fostering excellence in education, my former professor, Dr. Judy Carter, stands as a beacon of inspiration and mentorship in my life.

As a student fortunate enough to have been under Dr. Crater's tutelage, I was exposed to a pedagogical approach that transcended the conventional boundaries of teaching. Dr. Carter's teaching methods were not merely confined to the classroom; instead, they were a dynamic fusion of theory and practical application, encouraging students to not only grasp the intricacies of educational principles but also to immerse themselves in the transformative potential of those principles in real-world scenarios.

The skills imparted by Dr. Judy Carter were not just theoretical constructs but actionable tools that have proven invaluable in my professional endeavors. Armed with a profound understanding of educational psychology, curriculum development, and innovative teaching techniques, I ventured into the realm of education with newfound confidence. Little did I anticipate that these skills would be the cornerstone of my success in establishing and running a school for many years.

The foundation laid by Dr. Judy Carter transcends the conventional boundaries of education. It is a testament to the unwavering belief that each student is a unique entity, possessing untapped potential waiting to be discovered. Dr. Carter instilled in me the importance of fostering an inclusive and nurturing learning environment, one where students are not just recipients of knowledge but active participants in their own educational journey.

In the years that followed my time as Dr. Carter's student, I have had the privilege of witnessing the transformative impact of her teachings. The school I established stands as a testament to the enduring legacy of Dr. Carter's dedication to educational excellence. The principles ingrained in me during those formative years have not only shaped the ethos of my institution but have also contributed to the holistic development of countless students.

To Dr. Judy Carter, I extend my deepest gratitude. Your mentorship has been a guiding light, illuminating the path to educational innovation, compassion, and empowerment. This foreword serves as a humble tribute to a remarkable educator whose influence continues to resonate in the halls of learning and in the hearts of those fortunate enough to have been touched by her wisdom.

Sincerely,
Rebecca Terrell Dent
Founder
Charles Henry Terrell Academy

In 1987, I decided to change my major from Music to Early Childhood Education. It was then that I met Dr. Judy Carter. She was Chair of the Education Department, and although beautiful, she had a reputation as a no-nonsense professor.

I was desperate to change my major, but a little intimidated to take classes from Dr. Carter. However, this petite, beautiful, and intelligent lady became my favorite professor. She really was no nonsense, which was just what I needed to stay focused and do my best. I remember her telling me I needed to improve my handwriting if I was going to teach little ones. She insisted that I practice using children's writing paper. It worked, and although my penmanship is not perfect, it made me conscious of my handwriting when modeling for children.

It was not only Dr. Carter's honesty, and straightforward demeanor that gained her respect, but her genuine love towards her students that made me want to do my best and make her proud.

I recall schools reaching out to Paine College for its education graduates. They knew under Dr. Carter's leadership; the school was producing prepared teachers. When I graduated from Paine college in December 1990, I had many offers for teaching jobs. I started my teaching career in January 1991.

Today 33 years later, I accredit my success as an educator, principal, and now an employee of the Georgia Department of Education as a School Effectiveness Specialist, to Dr. Judy Carter. She taught me to always do my best and have a spirit of excellence. She modeled that not only in words, but the way she carried herself.

When I graduated, she invited me to dinner at her home and expressed to me how proud she was. That meant so much from someone who I respected so much. Her relationship, teachings and love will forever positively impact my life and career.

Affectionately submitted by,
Tonya Hankerson Bradburn (2024)
Paine College C/O 1990

Tribute for Judy Carter

It gives me immense pleasure to write a tribute to someone who is dear to me. I first met Dr. Carter in 1987 when I was a student at Paine College. I am from the Grand Bahamas. Before I knew her personally, my first introduction was when she gave a thought-provoking speech at our weekly Chapel services. Her overall demeanor and the way she spoke with such passion, admonishing students to take their studies in college seriously. As a guest speaker, she wanted us to fully embrace the opportunity we had to study and to remain focused.

I was able to know her on a more personal level when we travelled and attended Alpha Kappa Alpha Sorority, Inc, conferences together. She was the undergraduate advisor for our chapter on campus. She also became my college mom. In fact, I am her daughter. She invited me to assist with invigilation which was training grounds for me in the various posts I held in education. She coached me and guided me through all the leadership posts I held while at Paine College.

Her mentorship continued as I entered the workforce. All through my career, when I wanted to give up and sometimes became frustrated, she was the person who gave me the push to apply again. Every time I was successful in my promotion, she was happy and reassured me in my new role.

When I started working, I was able to call her on numerous occasions discussing challenges of life as a young professional new to the employment arena. Although the calls were long distance, she spent the time talking to me to hear me and to give me words of encouragement.

She is genuine and cares about my well-being, and of course, about the well-being of others. I do not know if she even recalls giving me an entire wardrobe. All the professional clothing that was my size and barely worn (brand new tags still on SMILE) she gladly blessed me with them. I had an entire professional wardrobe for work—thanks to Judy Carter.

When I was going to Paris to study French for the summer, she gladly told people that her daughter was in Paris studying. She made me feel special and I appreciate that.

My greatest admiration for Dr. Carter was the passion and professionalism she had for her work in teacher education. Her work in education, especially working with accreditation of Teacher Education programs across the United States, is commendable. I knew everywhere she was recruited to work. We talked about her various positions as she accepted them. Her work brought her joy because she wanted to see the Teacher Education programs thrive. She exuded extraordinary pride and joy in what she did.

Dr. Carter was a perfectionist. Everything she did she did with excellence.

Dr. Judy Carter is deserving of such praise and admiration. I am truly blessed to know her and to have spent time with her.

A Woman of Excellence!

Love,
JoyAnne Pennerman (2024)
Regional Education Director
Grand Bahamas

A Tribute to Dr. Judy Luchey Carter: A Legend in Education
By Dr. Jené Walker

When I first saw her, I knew she was legendary. She entered the class-room wearing a signature look that I would later attempt to emulate - a classic suit, heels, and a briefcase. I had never seen an educator, a pro-fessor, and the head of a department who was so elegant and beautiful. Then, she opened her mouth and the intellect matched her beauty and grace. It was at that moment that I knew I aspired to be like Dr. Judy Luchey Carter.

I am Jené Walker, an educator and business woman who graduated from Paine College in 1993. I had the honor and privilege of being a dual major in English and in Secondary Education under the direction of Dr. Carter and her amazing staff such as Dr. Laura Ann Grady. I attribute much of my success to Dr. Carter and her department which was one of the most effective and productive departments of educa-tion. She ran a 'tight ship" to ensure a quality education and sustain-able success for her students. One missing element in education is examples of legendary leadership. Dr. Carter, however, is the prototype for legendary leadership in education.

Dr. Judy Carter was extremely self-aware. She knew what she wanted and understood that not everyone would level up to her stan-dards of professionalism and collegiality. Dr. Carter always raised the bars of excellence. One of her standards was for all her students to pass the required certification tests before they ever graduated from the institution. The goal may have seemed lofty to some but it was an achievable goal. This goat not only enhanced the credibility of the department, but it required students to take their studies seriously and pass the test. It made us more marketable in obtaining student teach-ing and teaching positions.

Dr. Carter was friendly, fair, and firm. I could rely on her to con-sistently be the same for me and all her students. I recall an extremely uncomfortable situation during my student teaching experience. Dr. Carter came to my defense on the side of justice. She wore her signature look; she carried a briefcase to accompany her style and grace. Most importantly to me, however, she firmly expressed to the administration who I am and who she is - powerfully gifted and legendary educators. She let the administrative team know that if they did not appreciate my gifts, she could very easily place me in a school that did. She exemplifies everything I believe the Highest God ordained me to be. I was able to witness first hand a self-awareness mindset and authentic leadership in Dr. Judy Carter. She did not waver in her beliefs and core values because she is and always has been an authentic leader.

Dr. Judy Carter was purpose driven. She modeled for us how to be focused on how one's purpose will impact the masses. She knew her purpose was to transform education on a national level. Her vision reached beyond the campus of Paine College to educational institutions throughout the nation. I believe that my purpose driven mindset was impacted by witnessing Dr. Carter transform departments of education in whichever role she worked. If you trace her educational experiences, you will see a purpose map. She mapped out all her leadership experiences to fulfill her purpose.

If an institution needed accreditation, Dr- Carter was the one to call. Why? Because to accompany one's purpose, one has a repertoire of gifts. Dr. Carter mastered the gifts of leadership, administration, educational methodology and pedagogy, content, and curriculum development and so much more. Dr. Carter understood on a deeper level than most educators, what it takes for students to be successful in content mastery and in their educational careers. Because she knew her purpose and mastered the gifts required to fulfill her purpose, she is what I consider the quintessential example of a purpose driven leader.

Dr. Judy Carter had a transformative mindset and was what I consider to be a radical leader. She was one of the few leaders I have had who was willing to speak up and speak out. She was unconventional in her methodology. Even though I attended a smaller college and expected to be sheltered somewhat, Dr. Carter knew what we needed as education students. She knew that coddling us would not prepare us for some of the systems that are set up to fail us. Dr. Carter focused on creating departments that would have a lasting impact on the lives of her students. She did not level the playing-fields. She created fields that were unimaginable to most.

Dr. Carter was strategic in the design of each course, textbook, syllabus, and curriculum in her department. Her staff selection was strategic. Dr. Carter was not afraid to upset the status quo by imposing the highest standards she deemed necessary. Her investment in systems and in people were beyond surface level. She had a vision for molding and shaping legendary educators - even if it meant doing something radical in her time. If she needed to move from one city to another - she would do what she needed to do to effect change. I believe that remnants of her legacy still exist in the departments she pioneered.

Dr. Carter is my inspiration, mentor, role model, and friend. As a result of Dr. Carter's leadership, I have accomplished many great things. Under her leadership, I became Miss Paine College. Then, after my student teaching, I worked in two school systems as a teacher, K-12 Instructional Supervisor, and an Assistant Principal. After resigning from the school system, I established and built my own company. We are an educational support services company that creates leadership development books, workbooks, and curricula resources for educational departments in school systems, businesses, churches, prisons, nonprofits, and for students and parents. I recently graduated from Kingdom School of Ministry as salutatorian. I have not even scratched the surface of my own legend. There is so much more to come. Dr. Carter taught me to keep pouring and continue leading until I hear the Highest say, "Well done my good and faithful servant."

Dr. Jene' Walker, Management (2024)
Education & Business Consultant & Curriculum and Instruction Designer

2-3-91

Dear Dr. Carter,

I was very disturbed by your announcement of your resignation as Zeta Eta's graduate advisor. I suppose I should have expressed my concern last night, but I did not know what to say.

We are all surprised and saddened by your decision. I am hoping that the dispute between you and the graduate chapter can be resolved. If this chapter is in any way responsible for your decision, please forgive us.

Dr. Carter, I know that being our graduate advisor is a very difficult job, but please reconsider; even if it is just until May. It would be a tragic blow to all of us to loose you as our advisor in the middle of the semester. You are the most positive female influence I have encountered here at Paine College. You have truly tried to teach us about the meaning of an Alpha Kappa Alpha woman.

I will understand if you choose not to reconsider. You must do what is best for you. Please, always remember your work has not been in vain. You have made a lasting, positive impact on my life. I thank you and God bless you in all you do.

Love,
Shonda Collier

Colleagues Reflections

I am delighted to write this letter in support of Dr. Judy Carter. She and I met when we started teaching at Paine College in the fall of 1976. She was a professor in the Department of Education, and I was a substitute French teacher for Dr. Mallory Millender. Judy and I became instant friends because of our strong interpersonal skills. We found out we were from neighboring towns; she was from McCormick on the South Carolina side of the Savannah River, and I was from Lincolnton on the Georgia side.

When I returned to Paine College from a one-year leave of absence in the fall of 1980, Judy was no longer there. Nevertheless, she was away for only a few years before returning to the College as Chair of the Department of Education. (I was the Dean for Academic Affairs when she returned as Chair.) As Chair of the Department of Education, she assembled a quality faculty willing to work diligently in restoring the Department to its former glory of producing many leaders in the Richmond County School System and beyond. Not only did Dr. Carter work diligently to restore the State of Georgia accreditation to Paine's Department of Education, but she also achieved the same distinction on a national level by spearheading the efforts for Paine's Department of Education to be accredited by the National Council for Accreditation of Teacher Education.

Paine recognized Dr. Carter's diligence and commitment by selecting her as the recipient of both the Distinguished Teacher of the Year Award and the Evelyn Berry Teacher of the Year Award. Her very strong interpersonal skills and the quality of her service presented opportunities for her to work with all the surrounding school systems in placing both student teachers and teachers in their systems. Her work did not go unnoticed by others. She duplicated this effort with great success at Benedict College, Dillard University, Fort Valley State University, Livingstone College, and Voorhees University, all which attest to her unique ability to motivate, teach, guide, and extend overall support for faculty and students to reach their highest potential.

Respectfully,
Roger Williams, Ed.D.

Just Call Me Judy

Within weeks of joining the faculty of the department of education at The Fort Valley State University (FVSU) in 2003, I learned of the impending Professional Standards Commission review for accreditation. As a result of that review, FVSU lost accreditation. After two years of fruitless endeavors and leadership changes, newly appointed FVSU President Dr Larry Rivers determined to get the education programs accredited and running smoothly. Realizing that leadership was crucial to this happening* he reached out to someone he knew who had revitalized the education program at another college, one Dr. Judy Carter.

As is true in every faculty, some people were not excited about an outsider coming in to "show us how things could be fixed." Some were anxious about their role in the new regime; others were excited about the possibilities ahead. In our first faculty meeting in January of 2006, our new leader eased tensions by telling us to "Just call me Judy." And many of us did, as Judy made it easy for us to want to work with her toward common goals.

Getting reaccredited was not an easy task, and Judy soon found out just who was willing to put in the time needed. We worked WITH Judy Carter. We worked long hours, but if anyone was in the building working at 8 p.m., Judy was there with us. Having been through the accreditation process before, Judy knew that everyone on the faculty needed to be able to answer every question the review team might ask, so as we got close to the time to submit the documents to PSC, Judy led us in developing a process that worked for us. When a section was ready for review, the faculty gathered in the conference room, one person projected the document on a screen and one person read the document aloud. This meant everyone had input about the content, and everyone knew what would be submitted to PSC. This was very different from the 2003 review.

I would be lying if I said the process was smooth and that everyone worked equally hard. There were some who did not stay up until midnight reading the documents. There were some who did not show up on Easter Sunday afternoon to read more files. There were some who continued to try to do things the way they had been done "before Judy." But those people did not stay long after that first round of accreditation work. Judy was easy to work with, but she made it clear that if you did not want to work hard, if you did not want to change old habits for ones that proved their merit, if you could not contribute meaningfully to the department, you were not needed. There were some transfers and some resignations/retirements, but in the end, we were stronger for it.

Judy clearly believes that "All work and no play" does not lead to a happy workplace, so we included fun in our days. We often had refreshments at our faculty meetings, we frequently all went to lunch together, we even had a few craft workshops where we made special Valentines and gourd ghosts and pumpkins. We had swimming parties and off campus Christmas parties. After she had been there only a few months, we gave Judy a surprise birthday party, and this led to our trying to do something special bimonthly for birthdays.

I have had several bosses in my career, and the best ones were women who respected their faculty and believed in individual responsibility. They did not micro-manage, and they did not intimidate. They did lead and they did work WITH their faculties. These good leaders encouraged their faculty members to expand their personal accomplishments, to look for advancement and leadership opportunities, and to become leaders themselves. Judy Carter tops that list of admirable and respected bosses/leaders. I do not believe any of the successes of the faculty of the College of Education would have happened without Judy Carter leading us. Under her leadership, we resurrected education programs, developed

new programs, grew enrollment, developed new ways of working with students, and celebrated our victories. If anyone reading this needs a leader who knows how to get things done, my recommendation would be to "Just Call Judy!"

Eleanor K. Sikes, Ed. D (2024)

For Dr. Judy L. Carter

I met Dr. Judy Carter in 1993-94 at Dillard University. I am a graduate of Dillard U. with a major in Physical Education. Dr. Carter was recruited to Dillard University by Dr. Samuel DuBois Cook, President, in 1993, and had been on board for a short time before we met. Judy (is what she preferred to be called) had heard about some of the performances my dancers from St. Mary's Academy had done on Dillard's campus and brought me in for an interview. Dillard did not have a Dance Ensemble at that time, and she decided it was time to have one. She interviewed me and was elated to hear of my experiences in choreography in New York City, especially with Arthur Mitchell, Director of The Harlem Dance Theater. I showed her documents of performances I had choreographed and written reviews of shows. This was all she needed to offer me a position in the Department of Education as a P.E. teacher and Director of the Dillard University Dance Ensemble (the name I came up with). Mrs. Sylvia Cook, wife of President Cook, asked me to choreograph dances for plays she was writing. I did, and she, as well as President Cook, were pleased. Judy was also pleased with my work and often congratulated me.

Judy changed the Department of Education in many ways. One of her major responsibilities was to get the department ready for reaccreditation. She requested many upgrades for the department, and they were approved by President Cook. She professionalized the department and got it ready for reaccreditation, which the department later received. She was an inspirational leader, kind, considerate, and supportive. She encouraged us to do our best and be our best for the students.

As time went on, the Ensemble was catching on. With Judy's backing, I was ready to put on a showcase recital to show the Dillard community as well as the public what the Ensemble could do. I told her I would make everyone proud. Students put forth their best efforts to raise funds for costumes, tickets, and ads. The recital was a rousing success. The students were superb in executing the choreography and characterizations of "Let There Be Dance" Judy was over the moon and could not stop congratulating me or the production. And, of course, President and Mrs Cook were ecstatic. The entire audience could not stop applauding. The Ensemble took several bows before things settled down and everyone was invited to a reception after the performance.

Judy recommended me for the positions of heading the P.E. section in the Department of Education and Director of the Dance Ensemble. However, a new president was appointed, and he did not approve this promotion. He offered that promotion to someone of his choice. I sued and won, He also announced in a faculty meeting that major funding had been received since his appointment and Judy raised her hand and asked if any of that money had come from a black businessman in California. His response was "we will talk about that later in my office". According to Judy, that talk never took place, and the Office of Institutional Advancement informed her the gift of one million dollars she was responsible for, was received before the new president took office. They were told not to make the announcement, as he wanted to do that himself. Fortunately, his tenure did not last long at Dillard. Judy and I have remained friends over the years, and I will always remember her as a supporter, encourager, good listener, and friend. With all her attributes, her husband Jimmy is a lucky man.

There is a song that reminds me of Judy and every time I hear it, I think about her. The song is "I'm Every Woman".

Respectfully,
Elaine Smith, Retired Educator (2024)
Lafayette, LA

I have had the pleasure of knowing Dr. Judy Carter for over forty years and had the good fortune to work with her at Fort Valley State University when she was Dean of the College of Education, and I was an Associate Professor in the Teacher Education Program. Dr. Carter's reputation had preceded her, as I had heard about her ability to gain and maintain accreditation of teacher preparation programs at several institutions. When she came to Fort Valley State, the teacher preparation program was on the verge of loss of accreditation. She came in, assessed the needs of the program, built a cohesive team, and got to work addressing the challenges that the program faced. Within two years, the program had regained National Council for the Accreditation of Teacher Education (NCATE) accreditation. In whatever role she has served, from the K-12 classroom to executive administration at the higher education level, Dr. Judy Carter is and has always been the consummate professional.

Julius E. Scipio, Ed.D.
Dean of the College of Liberal Arts and Social
Sciences (Retired)
Savannah State University

My thoughts;

I am honored to write a few words about my friend and former boss, Dr. Judy Carter! Judy and I came to know one another at Fort Valley State University in 2008, when she, as Dean of the College of Education, interviewed me for a job. I was immediately struck by her professionalism, insights into FVSU, scholarship and her overall knowledge of the field of education. Even more important to me, however, were her listening skills, her sense of humor and genuineness as a person. Dr. Carter became one of the best, most supportive supervisors I have ever had in my many years in education and has remained a good friend over the years. As a well-respected scholar, she has enjoyed a variety of experiences in her career, and I continue to be amazed that she seemed to enjoy every one, diving into each with a positive attitude, am so eager to read the personal accounts of her professional and other life experiences. No doubt she will do so with intellectual insights and humor!

Your friend,

Jean Wacaster, Ed.D.
Chatsworth, GA (2024)

Judy Carter:

As a young professional entering a new venture with the Georgia Professional Standards Commission (GaPSC) after serving for over 10 years in P-12 education, I was confronted with a steep learning curve. I knew very little about the inner-workings of state government, and starting at the GaPSC exposed even more knowledge deficits that I had related to higher education and teacher preparation. Although, I had been prepared as an educator in Georgia by an approved educator preparation provider, it was quite a different experience being on the other side. Surprisingly, I quickly learned the fundamentals of program approval, including preparation rules and standards. Particularly when I started facilitating the approval reviews of educator preparation units and their programs. It was the process of assuring the application of program approval standards that proved to be invaluable. I quickly saw that those providers that performed well on standards were led by highly qualified and highly effective deans and chairs.

One such individual was Dr. Judy Carter. I was introduced to Dr. Carter by her favorable reputation in the field of education and throughout Georgia. In meetings, on task forces, and interactions with individuals in the field, Dr. Carter's name was synonymous with excellence, professionalism, and leadership. She was known as the clean-up lady, because she could take failing preparation units and make them over. When an EPP's performance status was in jeopardy, Dr. Carter was known as the leader that could turn an EPP's progress around. Dr. Carter knew the standards like the back of her hand as if they were written on the back of her hand, and more importantly she knew how to apply the standards by having the right drivers in place to assure quality.

Dr Carter was an effective dean and leader. One example is when she served as the dean at Fort Valley State University. Faced with complexities that are both unique and not unique to many colleges, schools or departments of education at Historically Black Colleges and Universities, Dr. Carter led her faculty and staff through a highly successful review. Dr. Judy Carter knew how to strategically build a strong team. She was the team's leader, but she was also a den mother of sorts, not tolerating excuses and underperformance. Her example of leadership positioned Dr. Carter as a mentor for many, including me. I wasn't a member of her faculty or team. I wasn't even the staff specialist assigned to Fort Valley State University at the time, but I knew as a young African American female professional, if I wanted to advance in my career, I had better align myself with strong female leaders like Dr. Judy Carter. The way I did so was securing her as a review team chair for an approval review I was facilitating as the state consultant. I knew she would lead the review with fairness and integrity, but I also saw it as an opportunity to observe her and befriend her. During a conference, I followed her closely making sure to engage with her to learn her secrets of being a phenomenal woman. What I noticed most was how personal she was. Everywhere she went during the conference, people would flock to her to say hi and ask for her advice. She carried herself like a queen or the President, but she was approachable, pleasant and polite. She was also firm, and she meant what she would say, and say what was on her mind.

In closing, Dr. Carter leaves a legacy. Even after retiring, she is still held in high esteem. At a recent conference, someone mentioned successful deans, and Dr. Carter's name was mentioned. I consider her a mentor, but also a dear friend. She will go down in history as a phenomenal woman, and pioneering leader.

Dr. PaQuita Austin Morgan (2024)
Program Durector, Georgia Professional Standards
Commission

Family Reflections

Judy Luchey Carter

As the husband of Judy Luchey Carter for the past 56 years, I realize daily, the wonderful gift that God bestowed on me as a lifetime companion, helpmate, best friend, lover, partner, caretaker, dutiful wife, mother, and supporter of all my endeavors, personally and professionally. Her devotion to our marriage has been, without a doubt, a miracle, and has been the sustainer of all that we have endured in our long marriage.

At the beginning, I first met Judy at the wedding reception for her marriage to her first husband. My family, at the time, was lifelong friends with the Johnson family of Aiken, S C, and thereby received an invitation to the occasion. My first wife, baby son, and my parents all attended the affair. During the course of human events, little did we have any idea of what God's plan was for either of us. After broken marriages that took place in both of our lives, it is indeed ironic that we would encounter each other some 6 years later under totally different circumstances. I was a science teacher At Levi White School, and Paine College placed her there to do her student teaching experience. I learned of her marriage ending, as had mine, so we had that one thing in common. As time and conversations continued, we found common ground in many areas of mutual interest. I finally asked her out for a date. She had a four-year-old son, Skip, and said he had to come along on the date with us. I immediately told her to bring him along as I was not about to miss that opportunity to enjoy her company. The date came off perfectly and thus began a 10-month courtship, which ultimately led to us getting married on February 10, 1968. My parents, upon meeting her and getting acquainted, immediately realized that she was good for me as a companion and fell in love with her. They were so pleased to know that she was to be a member of our family. My mother referred to her as her daughter thenceforth. In appearance, she was a beautiful lady, cute, extremely intelligent, confident, idealistic, independent, and possessed all the attributes anyone would be attracted to.

As a mother, Judy exceeded all expectations. She taught by example. She talked to Skip constantly about her life experiences, using appropriate language, standing up for your beliefs, the various matters of proper decorum, having respect for others, the pursuit of education, interpersonal skills and always being morally correct in all that you do. We totally supported all his involvements, and one of us, {or both}, was always present when he received his awards and honors for academic performance and his participation in the concert band. He exhibited above average intelligence, which was borne out in his scholastic performance, and was accepted as a presidential scholar at South Carolina State University. Today, she and Skip are remarkably close, and she is his primary confidant.

The journey began with us living in the house where I grew up. The house was old (1901) so Judy decreed that she would live there 5 years. After much planning and preparation, I was able to build an extremely comfortable home in the Belair Hills section of West Augusta. We enjoyed that home for 27 years.

I had an 11-year teaching career with the Board of Education, and 2 years in the military, before moving to a new career at The Medical College of Georgia. I was hired as a senior administrator and retired in 1997. After tenures with Paine (twice) and USC Aiken, she was recruited to, and accepted the position as Chair of the Education Department at Dillard University in New Orleans. After my objection to this decision, I had no choice but to capitulate and offer my support to her decision. The hand of providence was on her, and it took me a while to fully realize her true calling. She had much success at Dillard before being recruited to other colleges that needed her help. Meantime, Skip was now out of college and acquiring his own home, and well into his career at Savannah River Site (manager and senior instructor of Nuclear Physics and Math), so we decided to downsize and acquire smaller quarters for just the two of us. We found the perfect fit, after a brief search, at River Place Condominiums in downtown Augusta, where we have resided since July 1999. Judy continued her career at Ft. Valley St. University as Dean of Education. After 5 years, she retired and one week later was recruited back to Paine College to help with getting the Department of Education ready for reaccreditation. She agreed to help for one year but stayed three years getting the department ready, and reaccreditation was approved by the Professional Standards Commission of Georgia. After 3 years and two retirements, she was asked to come to Augusta University to Chair the Department of Education. She agreed to come for a year as Interim and help them find an appropriate chair. Even though the Dean of the College of Education wanted her to remain, after 1 year, I convinced her to retire for the third time, which she did. She has not worked full-time since.

Over the years, we had many wonderful experiences, such as traveling to many interesting places, both foreign and domestic. As Skip grew up, it was our intent to expose him to the world, so we would combine our vacations with the many business trips we both had and take him with us. My parents did this for me as a youngster and the lessons learned and experiences gained were invaluable as I grew to adulthood. We enjoyed organizations in which we were members, Broadway and Las Vagas Shows, museums, theater, the performing arts, resorts, beaches and the like. We stayed on the go as much as possible until the pandemic curtailed our travel and public events. My health has been in decline as I age and other situations slowed us down considerably, nevertheless, we still manage to travel as much as is humanly possible.

Our marriage has, as most do when people live in proximity, endured many difficulties over the years. They stemmed from our cultural background differences, financial difficulties in our early years, and disagreements over various issues as they would arise. Many times, our issues would be confrontational and contentious. We would eventually talk out and negotiate our differences until mutual understanding prevailed and peace was restored. It has worked for us, and we are still enjoying a wonderful togetherness as never before. We enjoy a deep appreciation for everything we have achieved, shared, and enjoyed together over these many years. Our memories are so precious and enduring.

As I write these lines, I am so thankful and blessed to have had Judy as my loving, enduring and caring wife for these 56 years. We celebrated our anniversary on February 10, 2024, with several close friends and family. It was indeed a humbling experience, yet joyous in realizing the milestone we had achieved. I am such a lucky man and to have had the good fortune to be married to such a remarkable lady. At age 81, she still exudes the regality and dignity befitting her station in this life. A life surely to be admired and emulated.

Our love endures,
James E. Carter, Ill. (2024)

Auntie Judy has always been someone that I admired throughout my childhood and into my adult life. Her life's story is a reflection of rising above unfavorable circumstances to become the accomplished and favored professional that she's proven to be in all areas of her life. One of the things that I've admired the most is the fact that she has always reached back to pull others up and help them along their journey. Whether it be support, guidance or direction that I needed, I knew I could depend on her.

Auntie Judy has always supported and encouraged all of my academic and personal endeavors. She never lets an opportunity go by without letting me know how proud of me she is by sharing my accomplishments with others. She's one of my cheerleaders and I'm equally hers as she never ceases to amaze me with the work she continues to do even in retirement. Even now in my career at Savannah River Nuclear Solutions, I can still see her influence on my life through my drive to continue to grow daily and to rise to new heights every day. Auntie Judy is undoubtedly a woman of poise and grace whose passion for helping others shines through from the moment you meet her.

Jana Chavous, MBA, CPSD
Senior SCM Program Specialist
Savannah River Nuclear Solutions

My Aunt Judy

The definition of development is the process in which someone or something grows or changes and becomes more advanced. I did not know this word would be instrumental to my upbringing and mean even more as I aged. As a youth, I did not have the knowledge and understanding of how having access to higher education and performing at the highest level would be this impactful. My Aunt has always been extremely influential when it has come to the development of higher education, especially amongst young Black Americans. I had always known that she held high positions in colleges and universities such as Paine College and Fort Valley State University, but what I did not know was that she was an integral part in reestablishing importance, prestige, and accreditation to those institutions.

With her knowledge and financial help, I was able to graduate from Aiken Technical College, with not one, but two associate degrees. I usually would gloss over my education before, but now, I understand how crucial it is to my development, not only in education, but in acquiring higher earning jobs. There is that word again, development. Growth is not achieved without it. My Aunt and this word are synonymous. I hope I have made her proud in all aspects of my journey. I want to let her know that her efforts, knowledge, and time were not wasted. Love you Aunt Judy,

Your nephew,
Marcus Patterson (2024)

I am Turetia Luchey, my Aunt Judy's 2nd oldest niece. My father was William (Sonny) Luchey, (deceased), her only brother. Aunt Judy has presevered in more ways than one in reaching her goals; now writing about her life, the ups and the downs along with the good and the bad. To my understanding, Aunt Judy was the first person in our family to attend and graduate from college. Because of her example, many of her relatives have attended and graduated college. I am so honored and proud to see Aunt Judy cross so many impossible roads, no matter how rugged they seemed. I salute you Aunt Judy!

Your niece,
Turetia Luchey (2024)

My Aunt, Dr. Judy Carter, has not allowed the dispositions of life, nor the disadvantages of not having much growing up, to distract her from having dreams. She overcame the distractions to become the best she could be as a mother, wife, and professional institute in her field of study in this not so nice society, because of her ambition and drive to have a better life. My Aunt Judy is a warm, thoughtful, yet precise person. Her accomplishments of having three college degrees as well as her involvement with her immediate family, extended family, and professional family, is commendable. She is very much loved and admired for her many accomplishments in life as well as her integrity as a person. I am very happy and proud to say this is my Aunt Judy, a dear friend when in need. I applaud you Aunt Judy; I love you and pray God's continued grace be in your life.

Love you,
Your nephew—William B. Luchey (2024)

Friends Reflections

*** Tribute To Judy ***

Picture a paragon of internal AND external beauty, integrity, compassion and loyalty, to name only a few characteristics of "Our Judy" which transcend decades and which I observed to compliment her journey early-on in our friendship! These of her gifts from God confidently grounded her, and by example, were infused into her students and those she mentored along the way. From an inter-relational vantage point, her humility and ability to easily become acclimatized in various educational settings has been her forte. At the core of the "unseasoned Judy" lies the same moral and dedicated framework which fostered her transition into the Dr. Judy Carter persona and effectively manifested themselves in her marriage, parenting, educational pursuits, and in her teaching techniques.

That she sets the bar high and weaves the standard of excellence into her professional, educational spiritual and personal life, speaks volumes to her impeccable track record.

The prongs of this author's journey were pondered by her—from the point of humble beginnings—WITH tenacity, to that of marked accomplishments—with humility. That meditation inspired her to pen her story, where her life's stages are masterfully interwoven into an appealing backdrop which promises a 'good read'!

As her friend of sixty (60) years, I am blessed, as well as enamored, by her calf for simplicity to those addressing her, wherein she demonstrates that the title of ED.d does not, exclusively, DEFINE who she is...thus, the sensuous birth of "Just Judy" I Love & many blessings in this endeavor...

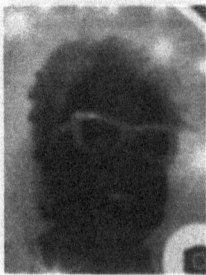

Friend forever,
"Tee" (TeVerra Chavous)

A Tribute to Dr. Judy Carter By

I recall meeting Judy at the time that she married my brother (Free Mason Johnson, Jr.). She was a bright light in my life, and I remember her as a sweet and loving sister (in-law). I didn't fully understand the commitment that she and my brother made, as I was only thirteen years old. Nevertheless, I loved her, and still do. I remember her fixing my hair for my junior prom, and on another occasion, she made a dress for me. However, the real impression came when she gave birth to my nephew (Free Mason Johnson, Ill). Later she became an educator, and I would become a teacher, also, and take a master's class with her as my professor. Judy is a wise and knowledgeable person who has helped so many people along her journey. I would like to acknowledge her continued love and concern, even after she and my brother parted ways. I wish God's blessings upon her, and her family, and am happy to have known her.

Margaret Johnson Sidney (2024)

A sisterhood began many years ago when my brother, Free Mason Johnson, Jr., married Judy Luchey. We liked a lot of the same music, hairstyles and clothing. Our conversations were smooth and easy. I am extremely proud of the child, Free Mason Johnson, Ill, that she raised to be intelligent man who has stella ethics. Dr. Carter created a legacy of educated young people who continue to serve our country in various capacities. It is my hope that they remember to reach back to bring other young people forward.

Ethal Ford (2024)
Detroit, Michigan

For My Dear Friend

Dr. Judy Carter and I met in 1989 at a sorority meeting, Alpha Kappa Alpha Sorority, Inc., Augusta Chapter. She was the undergraduate advisor for Paine College's chapter, Zeta Eta. I was new to the area, and she was so kind to me. We became friends instantly. Later that year, I was appointed undergraduate advisor for Augusta College's Mu Zeta chapter. Judy was pivotal in making sure I was aware of all the protocol that went along with being an advisor. We grew closer. I did not have a permanent job at that time and asked Soror Judy if she could assist me with finding employment, and she did. In fact, she made it possible for me to have several jobs I never would have dreamed of. I cannot put into words what she means to me. I do not think there is an adjective to describe her, but her husband would say, "She hung the moon." Her impact on our organization will always be cherished. I will forever tell everyone had it not been for Judy, I would not be where I am today in Augusta, GA.

With Much Love,

Desiree Herring (2024)
Richmond County Board of Education

Philippians 4:13 states, "I can do everything through Christ Who gives me strength."

Judy Luchey Carter, your life is evident of those Words for it shows you are a firm believer indeed.

Upon seeing and meeting you for the first-time during years 73-74 as a Consultant for the Title One Reading Program of the Richmond County Board of Education, I saw you as a 3-feet tall young lady in statue, whom I thought couldn't tell our group one thing, (LOL). Reason being, you appeared as if you had just graduated from elementary school yourself, (LOL). Once the Director of the program officially introduced you to our group of teachers, and you opened your mouth to begin to lecture, I feel that I could speak for all when I say we literally fell to the floor because this 3-feet tall young lady immediately grew to 6-feet within a five-minute period, (LOL).

I can't even tell you how quiet the room of 8 teachers became once Judy Carter began to speak. Suddenly, everyone, including myself, sat in awe while listening to this powerful voice of our consultant. Her voice was so powerful and without studder as she kept eye contact with us all.

At the end of Judy's lecture, the group had very few question since Judy had given the most effective training session ever. With me being a little quiet and reserved at this stage of my life, and being one of the newer teachers, I must say that Judy Carter encouraged, lifted and gave me confidence to continue on as a dedicated teacher. Her words of encouragement continue to resonate in my thoughts and my heart to this day.

Judy L. Carter, your success in life is so well-deserved due mainly to your obedience to God's Words. I will always thank Him for allowing our paths to meet, for with your unwavering Love for God, you're also a young lady of great wisdom, tenacity, generosity and authenticity.

Judy, as your friend, it would be an honor dear if you will please, "Step On Me", for I am so proud to call you "My True Friend for Life".

Ophelia Y. Adams (2024)

Dr. Judy Luchey Carter

Dr. Judy Luchey Carter is a very unique person. I met Judy when I worked at Paine College in Augusta, GA., and she was a professor in the Department of Education. She had, and still has, an authentic and humane attitude. Later when I was working as a teacher without certification, I took a course from Judy. Even though I knew her, I was a little afraid and shy in her class. I was a very outspoken person, but quiet in her class. She called me aside one day and asked why I did not talk up and express myself in class. She said because of my experiences, I had something to say and share with the class. She expected me to participate and not hold back.

I learned a lot about teaching from Judy. I used some methods and techniques which excited students to learn. Learning does not have to be boring. I also incorporated some of my own ideas to get the students to learn.

Later years, we moved into the same condo community and were reacquainted. We quickly became walking partners. We cherished our walks (early mornings) together while observing our surroundings, up and down the Riverwalk and up and down Broad Street.

Another thing that sealed our friendship was sharing a room at our Links Conference in Charlotte, NC. Judy took care of everything that involved our trip and gave me the receipts later. That trip gave us the opportunity to get to know each other better, and we had fun doing it. One of her outstanding attributes is taking care of others. She takes care of people and has that caring touch that makes people cling to her.

Your Forever Friend,
Mildred N. Kendrick (2024)
Retired Educator

Dr. Judy L. Carter

Judy Luchey Carter has been an amazing friend in my life. She has impacted my life in a way that has inspired me to be a positive influence to others. Her indelible footprints are difficult to fill.

I met Judy in the summer of 1965. She seemed unhappy and in a state of melancholy. Yet, she seemed to be goal oriented and was ambitiously striving to complete her Bachelors Of Arts Degree in Education from Paine College. We later became casual friends on campus. I was a freshman entering Paine and she was classified as a Junior. From Paine, she never stopped achieving and enhancing a career in education. She was unstoppable and eventually achieved a Doctorate Degree to teach others how to educate our youth. Judy has been a blessing to several institutions of higher education in the Historical Black Colleges and Universities (HBCU). Her training and guidance have successfully equipped quality educators throughout our country.

Judy's generosity is indescribable. She is the epitome of empathy, compassion, sharing, and caring. At church, Judy is a member of a Women's ministry, The Women in Christ. She goes beyond her call of duty to provide outreach ministry to the needy children, the Homeless, the sick, hungry, and the less fortunate. Judy is always eager to support Women's health, such as, the Breast Cancer Drive, Go Red for Women Heart Fundraiser, patients with Strokes, along with men and women in Nursing Facilities (Rehab Centers). She sets the example for giving of her time and monetary gifts. She generously donates to The Salvation Army, The Homeless students of the Central Savannah River Area (C.S.R.A.), The Ronald McDonald House, The Miracle Children Network, scholarships, and meeting any positive needs concerning youths.

Judy is very authentic and truthful about her God driven journey in this life. There is no shame in the hardships she has endured. She never took the path of least resistance. Through her belief in God, hard work, and generosity, Judy has risen above her challenges and adversities. She often expresses how grateful she is for God's continued blessings.

I am so grateful to God to have shared this walk in life with Judy.

To God Be the Glory for all the wonderful blessings He has bestowed in her life.

Brenda Johnson Hankinson, Retired Educator 2024

ACKNOWLEGEMENTS

WRITING A BOOK has never been on my bucket list. I only attempted it because so many of my former students as well as friends encouraged me too. I refused for 20 years or more until a few of them would not give up. They said I had a story to tell. So, two years ago, I decided to tell my story. Because I did not know how to begin, I called my friend and former colleague Dr. Leslie J. Pollard, Sr., and asked for advice on how to begin writing a book. I had read several of his published books. He did not hesitate and began advising me until I finished. I am grateful for his encouragement and concern and my deepest appreciation goes to him. I am also grateful to my husband Jimmy Carter, who supported me throughout this two-year journey. He provided hours and days of computer assistance and never complained. I thank my friend and Soror, Marlyn Dobson, who gave the book such an appropriate name and for writing the Forward. I began typing the manuscript myself and was making so many mistakes, I called on a church member and friend, Andrea Johnson, to help me. She retyped the manuscript in the order required by the publishing company, and I was able to submit it. I am deeply grateful to Andrea for coming to my aide.

I knew some things about my family but interviewed others to fill in the gaps. My brother's best friends, Curtis and Roosevelt Haskell revealed so many things about my brother that I never heard before. This information was invaluable. I interviewed my sister who also revealed things about my family I did not know. I spoke with persons in the Records Office in McCormick, SC, trying to get population statistics. When I was not satisfied with what they said reported, I spoke with persons at the Bureau of Statistics in Columbia, SC (the capitol of SC) for population statistics in McCormick from 1920-1942. The results were the same. I even searched Google for information on families in McCormick. I ended up visiting the McCormick County Library for information.

I acknowledge Palmetto Publishing Company for accepting my manuscript. I am grateful for your confidence in me as a first-time author. Finally, I want to thank everyone who submitted comments in chapter eleven, Reflections:

Kim Fender, and Joan Lamb, students at Windsor Spring Elementary School in 1967.

Stephanie Marquardt and Monica Tutt, students at Roy Rollins Elementary School in 1972.

Betty Tutt, parent of student at Roy Rollins Elementary School.

Nyleeche Green-McRae, Rebecca Terrell Dent, Tonya Hankerson Bradburn, JoyAnne Pennerman, Shonda Collier, students at Paine College from 1976-1980.

Dr. William C. Carper, Chancelor, University of South Carolina at Aiken.

Dr. Willaim H. Harris, former president of Paine College.

Dr. Samuel DuBois Cook, former president of Dillard University.

Dr. Burnett Joiner, former president of Livingstone College.

Dr. Albert J.D. Aymer, former Interim president of Livingstone College.

Dr. Larry E. Rivers, former president of Fort Valley State University.

Robert Bell, former Chair of Board of Trustees at Paine College.

Dr. Jeffrey R. Wilson, Office of Teacher Education, Columbia, SC.

Barbara Flemming Weston, Division of Teacher Quality, Columbia, SC.

Dr. Paula Dohoney, Associate Dean, College of Education, Augusta University.

Dr. Roger Williams, former Dean of Academic Affairs at Paine College.

Elaine Smith, Retired Educator (former instructor and director of the Dillard University Dance Ensemble).

Dr. Julius E. Scipio, Dean of the College of Liberal Arts (Retired) Savannah State University.

Dr. Eleanor Sikes, former professor in the College of Education at Fort Valley State University.

Dr. Jean Wacaster, former professor in the College of Education at Fort Valley State University.

Dr. Dill Gamble, former professor at Voorhees College (Retired)

Dr. PaQuita Austin Morgan, Program Director, Georgia Professional Standards Commission.

Dr. James E. Carter, lll., husband (Retired)

Jana Chavous,, niece, MBA, CPSD, Senior SCM Program Specialist at Savannah Nuclear Solutions.

Marcus Patterson, nephew.

Tureita Luchey, niece.

William Bruce Luchey, nephew.

TeVerra Chavous, (Retired Educator and friend for 60 years).

Margaret Johnson Sidney, (Retired Educator, friend and former sister-in law).

Ethel Ford, friend and former sister-in law.

Desiree Herring, friend and educator.

Ophelia Adams, (Retired Educator and friend).

Mildred Kindrick, (Retired Educator and friend).

Brenda Hankinson, (Retired Educator and friend).

9 798822 945876